"ICHIRO OZAWA has undertaken a far-reaching mission: no less than that of transforming the traditional Japanese way of thinking. He maintains that there must be profound changes in the Japanese ethos before Japan can fully assume the international responsibilities of a great world power. It must abandon the cherished concept of decision-making by consensus—which he believes has stifled political leadership—and give greater autonomy to the individual.

"This is a book that will stir much debate. But one can assume that that is exactly what Ozawa has in mind."

Henry A. Kissinger

"AN EXTRAORDINARILY important book. *Blueprint for a New Japan* provides a probing and incisive analysis of what is wrong with Japan's current political system and why a continuation of the status quo would be costly. It also lays out a bold, compelling vision of concrete changes that need to be made in order for Japan to function effectively as a major power in the world."

Daniel I. Okimoto
Stanford University

"A REMARKABLE BOOK. Mr. Ozawa does not skirt tough issues with mealymouthed clichés. His analysis of the challenges facing Japan is clear; his proposals for change are bold; and his affirmation of the importance of freedom central."

Michael H. Armacost
former U.S. Ambassador to Japan

"OZAWA'S PRESCRIPTIONS for reform are bold and comprehensive; his views will be controversial at home and enlightening to those who wish to understand modern Japanese politics and government."

Albert Carnesale
Harvard University

"A BLUEPRINT for a liberal reformation of Japan, Ozawa's book should be read by everybody with a serious interest in Japanese politics. More than that: it should be read by everybody with an interest in Japan."

Ian Buruma
author of *Behind the Mask* and *The Wages of*
Guilt: Memories of War in Germany and Japan

"OZAWA'S REFORM proposals and his call for a fundamental change in Japanese thinking should be required reading for anyone interested in the future of Japan and its role in the world."

Gerald L. Curtis
Columbia University

"THE VISION OFFERED by Ozawa is of a Japan that would put more value on individuals and innovation ... a Japan that the Clinton administration would also like to see."

Los Angeles Times

"OZAWA STANDS OUT as one of the few [politicians] with a sense of vision—for himself and Japan."

Time

"JAPANESE POLITICS, dominated by one-party rule for 38 years, has been shaken.... Now the world can read for itself, in this superb English translation, how the current upheaval in Japanese politics is part of Ozawa's sweeping plan to reshape the country."

Marjorie Sun
NATIONAL PUBLIC RADIO

"NOBODY TRYING TO UNDERSTAND Japan can afford to ignore this book. In 1993 Ozawa's ideas, backed by his forceful personality, brought about the collapse of Japan's postwar political order. In 1994 and beyond, they will be responsible for constructing a new order to replace it."

Sebastian Mallaby
THE ECONOMIST

BLUEPRINT FOR A NEW JAPAN

The Rethinking of a Nation

Ichiro Ozawa

Introduction by
Senator Jay Rockefeller

Translated by
Louisa Rubinfien

Edited by
Eric Gower

KODANSHA INTERNATIONAL
Tokyo • New York • London

NOTE ON THE TRANSLATION: *Japanese names have been rendered in the Western order, given name before family name. For clarity's sake, this translation uses "he/him" for non-gender-specific situations. The original text, like most Japanese writing, is gender-neutral.*

Published in Japanese by Kodansha as Nihon Kaizō Keikaku. *Some chapters have been adapted for the English edition.*

Distributed in the United States by Kodansha America, Inc., 114 Fifth Avenue, New York, New York 10011, and in the United Kingdom and continental Europe by Kodansha Europe Ltd., 95 Aldwych, London WC2B 4JF.

Published by Kodansha International Ltd., 17–14 Otowa 1-chome, Bunkyo-ku, Tokyo 112, and Kodansha America, Inc.

LIBRARY OF CONGRESS CATALOGUING-IN-PUBLICATION DATA
Ozawa, Ichirō, 1942–
[Nihon kaizō keikaku. English]
Blueprint for a new Japan / by Ichiro Ozawa: introduction by Jay Rockefeller : translated by Louisa Rubinfien: edited by Eric Gower—1st ed.
Translation of : Nihon kaizō keikaku.
1. Political planning—Japan. 2. Japan—Politics and government—1989–
3. Japan—Foreign relations—1989– 4. Japan—Economic policy—1989– I. Rubinfien, Louisa. II. Gower, Eric. III. Title.
JQ1631. 09313.   1994   320.952—dc20   94-14599 CIP

ISBN 4-7700-1871-1

Contents

Foreword 9

Introduction by *Senator Jay Rockefeller* 15

BOOK I THE URGENCY OF POLITICAL REFORM   19

Chapter 1   Overcoming Irresponsibility   21
Why Political Leadership Is Important
Staying on the Postwar Path, "Repeating History"
Reestablishing Competition for Power

**Chapter 2   Learning from Past Leaders: Ōkubo, Itō,
Hara, and Yoshida**   30
An Acute Sense of Mission
The Dangers of Failing to Exercise Power

Chapter 3   Defining the National Interest   36
The Legacy of "Defeat" in the Gulf War
The Government as "Corporate Lawyer"
The Politics of Indecision

**Chapter 4   Strengthening the Prime Minister's
Official Residence (*Kantei*)**   46
Introducing an Advisor System
Keep the Focus on the Prime Minister
Developing Comprehensive Coordination

Chapter 5   Integrating the Ruling Party and Cabinet   54

Are Bureaucrats the Decision Makers?

Bringing 160 Diet Members into the Government
   Administration

A Politician-Led Bureaucracy

**Chapter 6   The Advantages of Creating Small
Electoral Districts**   62

A Set of Four Reforms

Creating a Dynamic Politics

Political Contributions: 120 Million Observers

Policy-Centered, Party-Directed Election Campaigns

Diet Members Belong in the Diet

Chapter 7   Dividing the Nation into 300 "Municipalities"   76

Enacting a "Law on the Fundamental Principles of
   Local Government"

Let Local Governments Handle Local Affairs

A Transfer of Both Political Power and Financial Resources

Chapter 8   Wasting the Minds of Our Bureaucrats   83

Building a Crisis Management System

Fundamental National Policy

The Revitalization of Central and Local Government

BOOK II BECOMING A "NORMAL NATION"   91

Chapter 1   Japan's Role and Responsibility   93

What Is a "Normal Nation"?

The Costs of Peace and Freedom

The "Yoshida Doctrine," Misunderstood

Chapter 2   Toward a Peace-Building Strategy   101

Noblesse Oblige

Peace Maintenance and Japan–U.S. Cooperation

Reorganizing the Self-Defense Forces

Peace Activities and the Japanese Constitution

Chapter 3   U.N.–Centrism   113
Founders of a New Age
U.N. Management of Nuclear Weapons
Establishing a U.N. Reserve Army

**Chapter 4   Steering the World Away from the Trap
of Protectionism**   122
Aggressively Opening Our Own Markets
Creating a "World Trade Organization"

Chapter 5   An Asia-Pacific Ministerial Conference   128
An Accurate Recognition of History
"Flying-Geese Formation" Development
Five Guidelines for Japanese Foreign Policy
The Dawn of Multilateral Diplomacy

Chapter 6   Constructive Uses of Foreign Aid   138
An Aid Superpower
ODA as Part of Diplomatic Strategy
100,000 Foreign Students per Year
A Technical Training System for Foreign Workers
Leadership in Environmental Preservation

BOOK III THE FIVE FREEDOMS   151

Chapter 1   The Japanese Dream   153
"We Wouldn't Want to Be Like the Japanese"
Japanese Society Is Showing Signs of Strain
Becoming a Society that Values the Individual

Chapter 2   Freedom from Tokyo   159
30,000 Hours of "Commuter Hell"
The Limits of Unipolar Concentration
Housing for the Cities, Employment for the Provinces
Generous Investment in Our Residential Environment
Constructing a New Capital

Chapter 3   Freedom from Companies   171
Company Freedom, Individual Confinement
Going Beyond the Rapid Growth Era
The Severity of Individual Taxes
Cutting Income and Residence Taxes in Half

Chapter 4   Freedom from Overwork   180
Planning Our Own Futures
Three Reasons for Shorter Working Hours
An 1800-Hour Work Year

Chapter 5   Freedom from Ageism and Sexism   187
The Contributions of Senior Citizens
Senior Citizens in the Workplace
Increasing Choices for Women
Providing Pensions to Housewives

Chapter 6   Freedom from Regulations   197
Anachronistic Regulations
Toward a Rule-Based Administration
Companies, Individuals, and Responsibility

Chapter 7   Establishing Real Freedom   203
Democracy and Citizen Autonomy
Education that Encourages Independent Thinking
On Teaching

Foreword

I once visited the Grand Canyon National Park in America's southwest. Its 1,200-meter depth is truly awesome: more than four times the seventy-story height of Japan's tallest building.

To my surprise, I didn't see any fences. Multitudes of tourists come to the park annually, but no fences! I saw a young couple playing on one of the great boulders, but no park official was telling them to be careful. There wasn't even a sign to that effect. In Japan there would be fences, "no entry" signs, and park attendants who come running to warn people away.

I tried to imagine the scenario in Japan if an accident occurred. The press would criticize the park management in the harshest terms. The newspapers and television would demand to know how the authorities could have been so negligent—why there were no fences in such a touristed area, why attendants weren't keeping watch, why there were no signs. In Japan, park officials know what to expect and thus take every possible precaution. That is to say, they regulate our behavior. Any park visitor who obeys the rules can count on being safe.

Japanese people take it for granted that we are always under government protection—that even as adults, choosing our own pursuits in the freedom of our leisure hours, we are protected by some government office responsible for our recreation. Of course, America has its restrictions as well, but, fundamentally, Americans expect to take responsibility for themselves. Japanese prefer to have regulations not only to prevent accidents but to govern all societal needs.

During the recent economic boom years (the "bubble" period), Japanese liked to quip that their nation had a "first-rate economy and a third-rate politics." Those who, like myself, had made their lives in the political world were both frustrated and ashamed at the remark. But there was some truth to it. Just when Japanese companies were making great strides in the international arena, Japanese politics was mired in confusion, suffering a notable lack of leadership.

But at some point the bubble burst, and the business sector that called itself first-rate asked to be saved by the political leadership that it had derided. Since World War II—or indeed ever since the late nineteenth century—Japanese companies have prospered behind the protective shield of government, like small merchant ships surrounded by a mighty fleet. Companies competed with one another, but it was not free competition so much as a contest within a restricted area.

I don't think it is necessarily wrong for a society to favor regulation. There is no right and wrong in the nature of societies. But we must ask why Japanese society seeks to be regulated in this way. Japanese society is based on its particular history and traditions, and the Japanese people seek regulation because of these peculiarities.

Japan is a society that respects not majority rule but unanimous consensus. If even one person opposes a decision, it can't be made. If anyone persists in pressing his own opinion, nothing can be decided. The result is disarray. To prevent confusion, individual opinions are suppressed; everyone has to conform to the general consensus. Those who do not are quelled or ostracized. Conversely, though, in this consensus-based, village-type society, individual life and safety are protected by the entire community. Society regulates, and the individual who obeys the rules is guaranteed security and a relatively normal life.

Japanese-style democracy, then, might be defined as a system in which individuals are assured a secure life by the group in exchange for burying themselves in the group. There is no room in this system for the concept of individual responsibility to develop. This relationship between individual and society has endured because, with very few exceptions, Japan has historically been a homogeneous society with little contact with outsiders.

The initial efforts to change our society came in the Meiji period (1868–1912), when Japan opened its doors to the outside and, for the first time, introduced Western principles of democracy. Subsequently, however, with the failure of party politics and the ascendancy of the militarists, Japan once again fell into the dogmatic thinking peculiar to a homogeneous society. Dogmatic thought did not disappear with our defeat. The Cold War structure of international politics allowed us to continue to nurture our inclination for unanimous consensus. We do so even today.

But times have changed. "Japanese-style democracy" is no longer able to respond adequately to the changes taking place at home and abroad. We cannot continue to seclude ourselves. We must reform our politics, our economy, our society, and our consciousness, to bring them into greater currency with the rest of the world.

We can no longer enjoy the luxury of devoting ourselves exclusively to our own economic development, as we did during the Cold War. This is the main reason why we need to reform. If Japanese politics could once afford to confine itself simply to dividing up the wealth generated by economic development, that day has passed. We must learn to respond to the rapidly changing world around us, and do so with the peace and economic well-being of the entire world in mind. Our responsibility, now that Japan has become one of the world's leading economies, is greater than our people realize.

The second reason for reform is that Japanese society is itself becoming increasingly international. Increasing numbers of Japanese are living and working in foreign countries, and many foreigners are coming to Japan. The homogeneity that made "Japanese-style democracy" possible will soon be a thing of the past.

We need to change in at least three ways. We must first establish political leadership. We must ensure that the policy-making process is clear, and show our own citizens and the world who bears political responsibility in Japan, what they think, and what their larger visions are. Second, we must decentralize. Except where absolutely necessary, power should be transferred from the national to the local governments. We must respect local autonomy. Third, we must abolish excess regulations. We should preserve only the minimum number of rules necessary to govern economic and social activity, and adopt fundamentally laissez-faire policies.

The ultimate goal of these three reforms is the autonomy of the individual. Real democracy begins with this autonomy. Without it, we cannot be a truly free and democratic society. Nor can we be autonomous as a nation. People demand that our officials post warnings and build fences around our canyons. Individuals ask to be regulated; they renounce freedom. Local governments rely on the national government, and no one in the national government takes responsibility for political leadership.

Japan's most pressing need is a change in the consciousness of our people. Let us begin by removing the fences and educating the people to their own responsibility for themselves. We can encourage local autonomy through a decentralization of political power. Once political leadership is possible, we can expect politicians to take responsibility for their rule, and rely on the national bureaucracy to engage in creative, national-scale administration once it is freed from regulating the minutiae of daily life. Ongoing reform will be possible, too, once democracy and an awareness of individual responsibility are firmly in place.

In a sense, this book is intended as a prayer for that day. Many specialists have assisted me with it over the past two years. In today's political confusion, if this work can serve as a compass for the reforms that are needed in Japan, it will be a matter of great joy and honor to me.

Note to the American Edition

The intimate relationship between Japan and the United States has a long history. Japan's modern age began with the prompting of Commodore Perry's "Black Ships," which arrived in Japan's waters from America in 1853. Awakened by America from 250 years—or, in the larger sweep of history, from millennia—of isolation, Japan "opened" itself to the world.

Japan chose the new direction of "civilization and enlightenment" at that time, and worked hard to make up for the 250 years of lost time. The calls to build a "rich nation and strong military" and to "increase production and encourage industry" were powerful spurs to the people, who responded by eagerly absorbing American and European industrial technology. Our forefathers adopted Western political, administrative, and social systems as well. In some cases they took them on whole, and in others they adapted them to suit Japanese ways.

However, those who come rushing from behind always bear a certain handicap. In its anxiety to catch up with the West, Japan chose a course that had terrible consequences. Japanese and American interests clashed. The result was the Pacific War, followed by Japan's defeat. Japan's major cities were decimated and its industry destroyed.

Almost half a century has passed since then. Japan's economy has developed phenomenally over those fifty years, so much so that we are now called an "economic superpower." I feel great pride in this achievement because it is the fruit of each and every Japanese citizen's efforts. At the same time, we must remember that it was America's generosity and warm support that helped us rise from the ashes and rebuild our economy. We must never forget our debt of gratitude.

Today, however, a new and unwelcome atmosphere of friction has developed between our two nations. It takes the form of trade disputes. One of the many causes is that, in fundamental ways, Japan's markets are not entirely open to America and other foreign entrants. Japan is being urged to join the advanced nations of Europe and America by opening its markets in both name and reality. America is, in other words, pressing Japan to "open" its doors for the second time.

At the same time, the collapse of the Cold War structure has allowed long-suppressed ethnic and religious disputes to surface in and among many nations. Japan cannot remain a bystander as the world struggles with these new challenges. The question is what we should be doing. I believe that we must reaffirm the strength of our alliance with America. We must also work with the United Nations, which has new potential to be effective following the collapse of the Soviet Union. We should assume our economic, political, and military responsibilities to the world.

To assume these international responsibilities and to open our country, we must first reform our domestic systems and practices. This book is an attempt to explicate what reforms are needed and what their ultimate aims should be.

The first step toward a new political order came shortly before this book was published in Japan last June, when I and my colleagues split from the Liberal Democratic Party (LDP). In the following weeks, Japan saw its first transfer of power since 1955. The LDP reign ended, and a coalition government, which included our group, was formed. With the passage of the political reform bills at the end of January this year, Japan has taken another major step toward the kind of changes I have called for in this book. I am confident that the bills will become the springboard for further reforms in other areas, including economics, government adminis-tration, and foreign affairs.

I believe that it is my mission as a politician to work toward such a transformation. I am pleased and honored that this book is being published in America, and it is my hope that it can help foster stronger, closer ties between our two nations.

Introduction

by Senator Jay Rockefeller

Politicians in both Japan and the United States used the Cold War as a compass to steer their countries to a mutually profitable and remarkably stable relationship. For almost fifty years, the United States had a great interest in promoting a strong Japan as the front line against communism in Asia. And Japan had an equally strong interest in maintaining good relations with America as the market that fueled its economic growth. This relationship served us both well, and for that we should be grateful. Now, however, the end of the Cold War has meant a readjustment of our priorities and goals, and the political landscape has changed dramatically in both our countries.

The 1992 election of Bill Clinton, America's first president born after World War II, marked the beginning of a new era where our government could shift its focus from fear of imminent global conflagration to problems central to people's daily lives, such as creating more and better jobs for our workers, guaranteeing health care for all our citizens, and making our streets safe again.

Japan has also begun a new era in its political life. The 1993 election of a government *not* headed by the Liberal Democratic Party represented a monumental change in its political circumstances. The LDP, with its traditional power base of farmers and small shopkeepers, had a political lock on the Japanese Diet for almost forty years. The new government was elected initially to reform the political process, but the coalition victory was also a reflection of the erosion of the power of that traditional source of political support in favor of urban and suburban salaried workers. And underlying this change was the more fundamental question of how Japan must change to adapt successfully to the post–Cold War world.

One of the clearest voices in that debate is Ichiro Ozawa's.

15

Mr. Ozawa is not your typical political commentator banging on the walls of power from the outside. He is in fact the ultimate insider. He is a man who rose though the ranks of the LDP, and whose defection from the party signaled the end of its hold on power. He also played a significant part in getting the Hosokawa government's electoral reform package enacted, and he is committed to free and open trade.

Some may argue with the details of the plan laid out in his *Blueprint for a New Japan*. Nonetheless, I suggest that its ultimate aim—nothing short of a peaceful democratic revolution—is one that every reader should give serious thought to.

In this book, Ozawa proposes reforms on several levels: internal politics, international relations and, more radically, social attitude. On the political front, he calls for the establishment of real government leadership and responsibility in the formulation of policy decisions, both domestic and international. He also wants to decentralize government so that authority is transferred to regional officials. And he recommends that unnecessary controls and regulations be absolved to leave a minimum of rules to govern economic and social activity—a proposal consistent with the principles espoused some years ago by Prime Minister Nakasone.

The Japan envisioned by Mr. Ozawa is also a country that will play a role on the global stage commensurate with its economic clout. This extends to a variety of areas, from a more "hands-on" involvement in overseas aid development and environmental preservation, to participating in peace-keeping operations abroad. Ozawa wants Japan to work directly with the United States and international organizations to help maintain world peace and promote free trade.

For Americans, he envisions a Japan that will be more of an equal partner with the United States, one easier to deal with and more willing to share the burden of leadership. And for the Japanese, he sees a Japan that will allow its hard-working citizens to enjoy more of the fruits of their labors.

As a young man I had the privilege of living and studying in Japan. From 1957 to 1960 I went to school at the International

Christian University in Tokyo. I learned the language and developed many friendships there, some of which still endure and are a reason why I try to visit Japan regularly. The country as a whole in the early postwar period was a shambles. Housing had to be built quickly and cheaply, and the people had to work long hours to put their industry back on its feet. I was impressed with the hard work and dedication they brought to bear, and I admired their fortitude in extremely difficult conditions. But despite the fact that, in the years since then, Japan as a nation has made giant strides and become a world-class industrial competitor, I am far from alone in observing that its standard of living still doesn't reflect its extraordinary economic progress and strength.

Mr. Ozawa hopes to break this trend. He seeks a "Japanese dream" to rival the "American dream"—a dream that many may not personally achieve but that all can aspire to. And at the heart of Ozawa's "New Japan" is the individual. He believes that Japan must reorient itself to make the welfare of the individual the very basis of any reforms. To attain this goal, Ozawa has formulated the idea of five freedoms: "freedom from Tokyo ... freedom from companies ... freedom from overwork ... freedom from ageism and sexism ... [and] freedom from regulations."

If this reorientation occurs, it will have a profound impact on the future of the Japan–U.S. economic relationship. For years, while I have continued to express my regard for the Japanese people and their culture, I have felt obliged to criticize the country's unfair trading practices, its over-complex distribution system, and its protection of its own agriculture and manufacturing. Japan's government—both the politicians and the bureaucrats—has clearly been oriented toward the national corporations, and its citizens have traditionally subordinated their own needs to those of the corporations. By turning this situation on its head, as Mr. Ozawa recommends, the government would, by necessity, focus its efforts more on those who represent the new demographic realities in Japan and the changes that have occurred in the structure of its economy: the urban and suburban salaried workers. This sector of the population is relatively outward-looking and consumer-oriented, a new power base interested in improving its living conditions and in obtaining quality goods at low prices regardless of their origin. And these populist aims can only mean positive things for the trade balance between our two countries.

If Mr. Ozawa and people like him are able to empower the individual in this way, the desire to change will come from within: the people, as individuals, expounding their needs and wishes; bureaucrats, as individuals, expounding their own ideas and provoking competing ideas; and the politicians as representatives of the people responding to the needs of their constituents. These concepts are fundamental to Americans, but they will require the Japanese to accept less predictability and broader responsibility for the country's direction.

I believe that foreign readers in general will get great value out of this book because, in describing his path to reform, Ozawa explains the Japanese way in a manner that makes it easy for people who are not experts on Japan to understand where its stands today, where it came from, where it may be heading, and why it must change. Japan played a remarkable role in the postwar era; it rebuilt its economic infrastructure in an unprecedented manner and became a trusted member of the community of nations. Today Japan is at a crossroads. The Cold War is over, economic growth has slowed, and the underlying socioeconomic structures are showing signs of strain. In the future, Japan will certainly change—the question is, how? *Blueprint for a New Japan* presents a plan for how that might happen.

I am deeply heartened by this book because it shows a prominent politician stepping out of his appointed role to stimulate a timely debate on serious issues concerning Japanese life and politics. He makes his own contribution by suggesting answers that would require changes in policy *and* philosophy. And he offers a future with benefits not only for the people of Japan and the United States, but for other nations around the world.

THE URGENCY OF
POLITICAL REFORM

Editor's note

This book was published in Japan in June 1993. Since then, Japanese politics has seen many changes. The Miyazawa government, for example, is no longer in power, and the ruling LDP, in power for decades, has become the opposition party. In Europe, the EC is now the EU. However, because some of the discussions are situation-specific and because in some ways *Blueprint* is a document of its time, terms and tense have been left unchanged.

Overcoming Irresponsibility

Why Political Leadership Is Important

Weak political leadership is, for most nations, a domestic concern. However, once a nation has grown so powerful that its every action carries international ramifications, lack of leadership is an impermissible luxury: it is nothing less than an imposition on other countries.

Japan now accounts for 16 percent of the world's gross national product (GNP), second only to the United States. Together, the two nations comprise almost half of world GNP. Along with Europe and the United States, Japan is one of the major pillars on which the world economy rests. Japan's slightest move has an impact that reaches every corner of the globe.

Like it or not, it is clear that Japan has become a global power that cannot avoid the responsibilities that come with power. Cold War–era Japan was content to leave world matters in the hands of the United States, but present-day Japan can no longer do so. Strong leadership has clearly become imperative for Japan, but does it have that leadership?

George Kennan, historian, diplomat, and architect of America's Cold War policies, once compared pre–World War II America with the dinosaur. America, suggested Kennan, already had vast influence in the world, but, like the great beast with its tiny brain, had not learned to exercise sufficient control over that power.

Today, the analogy aptly describes Japan. As an international power, Japan has a global responsibility to frame active, comprehensive, long-term, dynamic, and consistent policies. But in fact we continue to devise only policies that are passive, partial, and short-term, and even these tend to be the product of last-minute decisions. Japan has become the ultimate "dinosaur."

The Japanese political system is based on a parliamentary-cabinet structure in which the ruling party and the cabinet together govern the nation. Because the leaders of the Diet (Parliament) and of the executive branch of the government are the same people, Japan has one powerful entity running the country, unlike the United States, where the legislative and executive branches are separate. The prime minister, at the top of this structure, is in theory all but omnipotent. However, in reality, as we know, the prime minister has proven anything but omnipotent.

Why this gap between formal and actual power? The peculiar circumstances of postwar Japanese politics explain the disparity.

Almost half a century has passed since the end of World War II. During this period, Japanese politics has had only one role: the supervision of the fair distribution of the wealth generated by the hard work of the citizenry. Politics, in other words, has been reduced to the task of apportioning the dividends of "Japan Inc." It is not my intention to criticize this. Given the conditions in early postwar Japan, it was in some ways the most important responsibility politics could have.

Japan's economy at the end of the war was in ruins. Japan became an important strategic base for the United States in a world dominated by the Cold War. It was in light of these conditions that Prime Minister Shigeru Yoshida decided on a political strategy giving domestic economic recovery priority over international politics.

The problem arose in the politics of later years. The economy overcame the chaos of the postwar years and experienced tremendous, high-speed growth. Unfortunately, the same cannot be said of politics; its role remained unchanged. It has kept its focus on apportioning the national wealth. Despite the end of the Cold War, no effort has been made to change this, and Japan therefore remains unlike "normal" nations. We continue to receive and not to give, surviving, as it were, on a single lung.

Postwar Japanese political leaders left to America the larger responsibility of formulating foreign policy, and concentrated on spreading the domestic wealth. Strong leadership was not only unnecessary but unsuitable to the fair distribution of wealth, which rested on mutual dependence and compromise. The result was a politics of complete consensus. The only decisions that could be made were those that somehow included everybody. It is this consensual politics that has enabled the Liberal Democratic Party to remain in power for nearly fifty years, and that has similarly enabled the Japan Socialist Party* (JSP) to remain the main opposition party throughout this period. Ironically, despite the powers guaranteed by the parliament-cabinet system, the LDP imposed on itself the restraints of political consensus, ultimately costing the party both leadership and power. It is my belief that the LDP is caught in a trap of its own making.

The main cause of the lack of leadership in politics is this extreme diffusion of power. Although power is technically concentrated in the office of the prime minister (who is also, by definition, president of the ruling party), power in reality is divided between the party and the government (prime minister and cabinet). This arrangement might be permissible if the party and the government each took firm leadership in its own sphere, but neither does. The LDP, for example, is divided into a handful of factions. It lacks unity, and serious matters of policy tend to become little more than tools in factional haggling, as was all too evident in the recent struggle over political reform. As we will see, the government, for its part, is also fractured.

Staying on the Postwar Path, "Repeating History"

A second problem is that the policy-making system lacks coherence. The policy-making processes of both the LDP and the government are highly diffuse.

The LDP's Policy Affairs Research Council—which ostensibly directs party policy—is actually an assembly of diverse and special interests. Its *bukai,* or committees, are divided along the lines of the bureaucracy (finance, commerce, transportation, etc.) and act in cooperation with their bureaucratic counterparts. The formal institutions that exist to coordinate the whole are not, in fact, effective.

The government, meanwhile, is itself scattered among many institutions and interests. Its ministries and agencies are discrete entities. No overarching institution exists to coordinate and control the whole. The cabinet, of course, technically plays this role, but it has never actually been expected to do so and has therefore never developed the necessary procedures. Put another way, the hands and feet of the political structure were created, but the "brain" to govern them was not. Japan's political framework is a strong parliamentary-cabinet system in name only.

Numerous problems result. The cabinet meeting, for example—nominally Japan's supreme decision-making body—is an empty institution. Substantive debate does not take place. "Final decisions" are made in advance, and the cabinet meeting is reduced to mere ritual. The same can be said of the Council of Vice-Ministers, where the highest levels of the central bureaucracies meet. Since no decisions are made there either, the council meeting is also just a formality.

In point of fact, it is not entirely clear just where decisions *are* made. It is hard to surmise how the various policies of the relevant offices are integrated, who is making what decisions, or where they are made. Policy, in other words, is decided without anyone's taking responsibility for it.

Thus the hands, feet, and tail of the dinosaur that is Japanese politics accommodate each other; the beast moves, but without a clear direction or priority. This could be described kindly as a "grass-roots" decision-making process, a term that makes the process sound distinctly democratic. And it may in fact have served commendably in a period of little change. But we will fail to respond to the tumultuous changes that lie ahead if the decision-making process continues to be so convoluted that we cannot decide on a single course.

We must develop a comprehensive, strategic decision-making apparatus that is firmly focused on the real and pressing issues facing Japan. At present, no such apparatus exists.

America here provides an extreme contrast to Japan. As I understand it, the president is presented with a number of policies that have already undergone thorough scrutiny, from which he selects. At least this is the ideal American leaders strive to achieve. The Japanese prime minister, however, does nothing of the kind. By the time a plan reaches the prime minister, all the ministries involved have resolved their own procedural details. And since no one is responsible for overall policy, the real objective of the policy has been obscured. The prime minister is nothing more than master of ceremonies for the ritual at hand.

This lack of real leadership is not only burdensome to our foreign counterparts, it is also dangerous for Japan itself. Prior to World War II, Japanese policy making was frequently immobilized because the army and navy were at loggerheads. The army insisted that the most likely future enemy of Japan was the Soviet Union, while the navy was emphatic that it was the United States. The two sides overcame this impasse by compromising and agreeing to regard both America and the Soviet Union as likely enemies, a solution that was obviously the height of absurdity. But without any institution to set fundamental national policy, Japan was pulled along by the willful actions of its hands and feet, and the result was this lunatic decision. Again, it was lack of leadership that ultimately permitted the military to act so recklessly. The fiasco that resulted was, of course, World War II itself.

Today, those who object to the contribution of troops and other personnel to international peace-keeping efforts argue that Japan must adhere to its strict postwar refusal to send military personnel abroad. To do otherwise, the argument goes, would be to retread a familiar and tragic path. In truth, we do actually risk repeating history—but it is by our *lack* of leadership, by our *inability* to make political decisions that this is so. If we remain unable to make decisions, we will simply be dragged along by events; we will fail to make even humanitarian contributions to the outside world, and Japan will find itself isolated from the international community. Isolation is where the true danger lies. The "history" we dread repeating would be Japan's failure to cooperate with Britain, the United States, and the other nations of the world. We must not forget this history.

The fundamental aim of political reform must therefore be to consolidate in both form and substance the democratic authority that has become so dispersed, so that we can give those nominally in charge both the responsibility and the power to make the necessary political decisions.

Reestablishing Competition for Power

A third major weakness of our political structure is the absence of competition for power. Competition has not always been missing. Early in the postwar period, intense competition for power was the norm within the ruling LDP. The prime minister/party president won his seat on the support of a multi-faction majority. He then selected the party secretary-general and, frequently, the finance and foreign ministers from within his own faction. The party president and his faction therefore bore responsibility for decision making and implementation of policy. Since opposition factions within the LDP were vying for power as well, the ruling faction was subject to severe criticism when it failed to meet its responsibilities. This was of course merely an intramural contest, but it was a contest nonetheless. The competition ensured that a variety of social concerns and needs would be addressed.

However, as the economy surged, LDP factions no longer had to vie for scarce resources to parcel out; there was plenty to go around. By the 1980s, competition had ceased altogether. In its stead the LDP developed what it euphemistically called "harmonious politics." Every faction became mainstream, and the governing principle became unanimous agreement, whatever the issue.

This meant that the responsibility for any policy failures lay with everyone and with no one.

Affluence has eliminated the drive to compete. LDP factional politics focused on dividing the spoils of economic growth, but we have reached the limits of this excessively narrow view of politics.

The end of intra-LDP competition would not be a very serious loss if the ruling and opposition parties competed for power, but that struggle, too, has disappeared. It is true that the opposition parties put on a bold show. They dig in their heels and vow to resist the government to the bitter end. Behind the scenes, though, they are making deals with the LDP; the parties negotiate their respective points of interest and together reach a compromise. Majority rule, meanwhile, is denounced as an abuse of power. Unanimous consensus has—much to the detriment of the national interest— become the overriding principle.

What are the consequences of this pursuit of consensus? The process by which the Peace-Keeping Operations (PKO) bill became law in 1992 illustrates how excessive consensus actually undermines the democratic principle of majority rule.

The major member nations of the United Nations have for many years participated fully in peace-keeping operations. The government's initial (1990) proposal for the recent PKO bill stopped short of this. Japanese participation was to be restricted to noncombat missions and subject to other special conditions. The bill was then diluted further to meet the demands of the smaller opposition parties, the Kōmeitō (Clean Government Party) and the Democratic Socialist Party (DSP). But the JSP declared that Japan's activities must be limited to such activities as overseeing elections. In other words, the Socialists denied PKO participation in any form the world would recognize as significant. The JSP then announced that it would boycott further deliberations on the bill if its proposal was not accepted.

In sum, the governing party was told to make further concessions, even though compromise had already gained it a majority in both houses of the Diet. The LDP was effectively forced to compromise until unanimous agreement could be reached. The media, in keeping with their role as pillars of the politics of consensus, did not question the behavior of the opposition. In fact, the major newspapers and television networks insisted that the Diet pursue consensus for as long as the deliberations lasted.

Let's suppose that the government, driven into a corner by the JSP and the media, had made such significant concessions to gain JSP consensus that it distorted its own fundamental position. What would have been the result? The proposal that had already gained the support of a majority in the Diet would have been changed entirely to mollify a minority that acted like a group of spoiled and fretful children. "Unanimous consensus" turns out to mean the tyranny of the minority.

But what happens when policy fails? Who takes responsibility, the majority that holds government power or the minority that does not? It is easy to imagine a scenario in which the majority is so repelled by the spoiled-child act of the minority that it avoids decision making altogether. Who takes responsibility if this inaction has negative consequences? No one can. We might call this the tragedy of an excessive pursuit of consensus. Postwar politics in Japan has undervalued, even ignored, the principle of majority rule. The result has been a politics without responsibility.

Again, all of this was sufficient as long as the Cold War structure supporting it was in place. The international environment permitted Japan to be a nation that did not function independently; that was Japan's place in the world. It is now imperative that Japan build a system in which those who have been democratically delegated authority take responsibility for decision making.

It is not enough simply to strengthen governmental power. Power must be strong, but it must also have clear and appropriate limits. It must not be so scattered that it is unable to devote itself to its top priorities, nor so omnipresent that it creates a body of citizens who are excessively dependent on authority.

How are we to limit power? Exhaustive discussion pursuing consensus is clearly not the answer. Rather, we first need to reduce the burden carried by those in power. Anything that does not absolutely require intervention from the central government should be transferred over to local governments. In addition, we must limit power by ensuring that the government periodically changes hands. We must discard the ill-defined powers and policies that seem to stay on and on for no good reason. Instead, we must have a government that takes responsibility for a fixed period of time, for clearly defined powers and policies.

With these limits firmly in place, we must see to it that the necessary power is concentrated in the government on democratic principles, and that competition takes place for that power. This is the way to endow Japan's large and able body with a genuine "brain."

---

* The Shakaitō changed its official English name to the Social Democratic Party of Japan in 1991. The Japanese name remains Nihon Shakaitō, or Japan Socialist Party.

Learning from Past Leaders: Ōkubo, Itō, Hara, and Yoshida

An Acute Sense of Mission

Japanese are generally fearful of the concentration of power. We prefer to stumble along, leaning on each other in what could be termed the politics of collective irresponsibility. This is clearly inconsistent with modern democratic thought. Competing policies, the clear demarcation of responsibilities for decision making, transparent rules that govern exchanges of power: these are the forms of power truly founded on democratic principles.

In our own modern history, four leaders—Toshimichi Ōkubo (1830–78), Hirobumi Itō (1841–1909), Kei Hara (1856–1921), and Shigeru Yoshida (1878–1967)—stand out for their ability to pursue bold nation-building efforts amid the dramatic historic changes of their times.

Toshimichi Ōkubo played a major role in the 1868 Meiji Restoration that ended 250 years of feudal rule under the Tokugawa government. He led the movement that abolished the feudal domains and figured prominently in the establishment of a prefectural system. He founded the Home Ministry and, as its first leader, laid the groundwork for the industrialization of the nation. When debate arose about sending troops to Korea, he resolutely opposed military action and crushed the movement to dispatch troops. He also helped quell the Satsuma Rebellion of 1877, the most serious anti-government uprising of the period. He was thus a major

30

architect of the centralized state and helped construct the very foundations of the modern Japanese nation.

Hirobumi Itō forged Japan's cabinet system, became the nation's first prime minister, and drafted the Meiji constitution. He also promoted revision of the unequal treaties with foreign powers to assure Japan's independence.

Kei Hara, in his post as chairman of the Seiyūkai Party, headed the first party-led cabinet. Under his leadership, parties became an established part of Japanese politics and were key in formulating domestic and foreign policy in post–World War I Japan.

Finally, Shigeru Yoshida, whose power was based in the pro-Anglo-American camp and in the bureaucracy, negotiated with GHQ (the General Headquarters of the Allied Powers, which presided over the occupation of Japan) to achieve the myriad reforms that followed World War II. Yoshida's work was instrumental in assuring Japan's peaceful independence.

These four men were exceptional individuals. They had a firm grasp of the political system, built strong power bases, and demonstrated superior leadership. Yet these very qualities earned them low marks from their contemporaries, because Japanese-style democracy favors leaders who emphasize consensus.

This is evident in the way their careers ended. Ōkubo and Hara were criticized for their "high-handed" politics, and both died at the hands of terrorists while still in office. Itō, who held numerous newly established posts including that of prime minister, was ultimately promoted to the Privy Council. He was assassinated some time later. Yoshida, too—surrounded by political enemies while serving as prime minister—was forced to use all his political capital to provide leadership in his post, until finally he sacrificed his political life.

What enabled these men to exercise such strong leadership? All shared an intense consciousness of the national interest, a sense of mission, and the will to use the power they had. They were subject to severe criticism from all sides, but were focused on fulfilling their missions. They held firm command of the reins of power and were not afraid of strengthening them where necessary to ensure the implementation of their vision.

Ōkubo, for example, was censured as an "autocrat" and accused of abuses of power. Undaunted, he maintained his efforts to consolidate in the central government the power that had previously been so dispersed. Ōkubo understood that constitutionalism is, in principle, the just and proper path, but he was acutely aware that the paramount issue for Japan during this time was to "catch up" with the advanced nations of the world. He was convinced that Japan could achieve this goal only if the government bore complete responsibility for every aspect of policy. He therefore set about creating a powerful, centralized government and threw his weight behind the Satsuma-Chōshū (the leading factions in the Meiji Restoration) alliance. He has been accused of aggravating the concentration of power in Satsuma-Chōshū hands, but it is important to recognize that this was the power base that enabled the government to modernize Japan.

Hirobumi Itō, who served as prime minister several times under the Meiji constitution, was sometimes criticized for introducing a system that put cabinets above party control. Yet he anticipated that the support of political parties would prove indispensable for domestic political stability, reversed his earlier opposition to parties, and founded his own party, the Seiyūkai. When his original source of support, the Satsuma-Chōshū alliance, dissolved as a result of his actions, he fortified his support within the Chōshū faction even though it meant antagonizing his former Satsuma ally, Aritomo Yamagata. Itō, born to the regional and factional politics that dominated the 1870s and 1880s, developed new power bases as needed in a flexible response to the changing times.

I feel a particular fondness for Kei Hara, partly because we were both born in Iwate Prefecture. As the successor of Itō and others, Hara was the first Seiyūkai chairman to have been born and raised, in a career sense, within party circles. His ambition was to bring both politics and government under unified leadership, namely that of the Seiyūkai. He not only received an absolute majority for the Seiyūkai in the Lower House, but also saw to it that the committees and study groups in the Upper House were firmly under pro-Seiyūkai leadership. He solidified Seiyūkai support in the Home Ministry and named Seiyūkai members to the posts of army, navy, and justice ministers. With a strong power base in place, he was able to restrain both the Satsuma and the Chōshū factions and pave the way to an era of friendly relations with the United States in the 1920s.

"What if …?" questions do not help us in the study of history, but I cannot help believing that if Hara had not been assassinated in 1921, he might have ensured the exercise of firm political leadership by the parties over non-democratic elements. Shōwa history might have been utterly different as a result.

Shigeru Yoshida's Liberal Party scored a decisive victory in the general election of 1949. Yoshida nevertheless had the foresight to plan the powerful postwar conservative union of the rival Liberal and Democratic parties, thus creating the LDP. His strategy flowed from his vision of a democratic Japanese state. He recognized that a democracy would prevail only if conservative factions set aside their differences to fight the more fundamental battle between liberalism and socialism. He built on the strength of the nascent conservative alliance, exercised fully the power authorized to the prime minister by the new constitution, and thereby laid the foundations for the prosperity of the postwar period.

The Dangers of Failing to Exercise Power

Why were these four leaders able to strengthen their bases of power in the face of constant and severe criticism? I believe it is because they recognized that, in Japanese politics, even the most exceptional and effective of leaders can do little without a solid power base.

A point of particular interest here is that the Shōwa period (1926–89)—in contrast to the previous sixty years beginning with the Meiji Restoration—produced only one example of firm leadership. It was in this sense a barren age. The prewar and wartime

Shōwa years saw the repeated failure of efforts to establish strong leadership. The post-Yoshida period did not even see the attempt. Shortly after the war, the so-called "1955 system" took root with the emergence of the conservative LDP and the left-wing JSP. During the remaining thirty-five years of the Shōwa period, these two parties stood firmly in place and mutually dependent. Strong leadership was not in the least desired, and therefore not forthcoming.

A few prime ministers, of course, aspired to real leadership, even under the 1955 system. However, the more entrenched the political framework became, the more rigid and even fossilized the LDP's administrative organizations and personnel became. The prime minister was rendered ever more powerless as a result. How, then, are we to break through today's political paralysis and establish the kind of prime ministership that can lead Japan into the twenty-first century?

The four politicians discussed above provide us with outstanding models. Each began with a clear vision of Japan's place in the world, and demonstrated the necessary will to strengthen and expand his political power base. Ōkubo bolstered the Satsuma-Chōshū alliance; Itō recognized the limits of that alliance and embarked on political party formation; Hara expanded the power of his party, the Seiyūkai; and Yoshida exercised to the fullest the powers available to him as prime minister and steered the Liberal Democratic Party.

We need a new and heightened awareness of the powers accorded the prime minister by the present constitution. By "awareness" I do not mean the passive consciousness that focuses on the limits on power in a democracy. Rather, it must be an active consciousness that seeks to liberate the power of the prime minister from the empty rituals and harmful habits that developed under the closed 1955 system. Instead of defining only what the prime minister must not do, we need to develop a vision of what it is the prime minister *must* do. It is essential that we learn from our predecessors.

There will be no shortage of objections to what I am saying. But

I am willing to expose myself to considerable criticism and risk because, among the many "dangers of power," there are both the dangers of exercising it and the dangers of failing to exercise it. Thus far we have recognized only the threat of excess power. The political immobility we face today is indicative of the dangers inherent in not exercising power.

The administrative organizations that today penetrate every part of society are divided and subdivided into highly specialized concerns. Left to themselves, they tend to become only more disparate and scattered, with the result of paralysis in the administrative and political worlds. But the primary cause of our political impotence has been our tolerance; we have allowed the prime minister to get away with not exercising the power of his office.

In Diet deliberations during the Persian Gulf War, for example, the Cabinet Legislation Bureau sometimes asserted its own views in contradiction to the official position of the government. Ostensibly, of course, this office pleads the government position in Diet questioning. It failed in its responsibilities and, by all rights, should have been punished. Autonomous action by discrete parts of the government immobilizes both its political and administrative functions.

The prime minister needs principles that serve as a compass in guiding the nation if he is to exercise real leadership. He must also have the means to apply those principles to concrete issues. That is to say, he must have constant and comprehensive access to accurate and up-to-date information. Historically, prime ministerial support systems have been expanded after the administrations of such men as Ōkubo, Itō, and Hara, probably because it was recognized that a strong prime minister must have sufficient backup.

Today, we face rapid and dramatic change. The prime minister should be a politician with a clear sense of mission, the will to exercise authority, and the courage to carry out his ideas. Moreover, a system-wide reform will be indispensable if the prime minister is to have the support necessary to lead effectively. These are the lessons we should learn from the greatest leaders of our modern history.

Defining the National Interest

The Legacy of "Defeat" in the Gulf War

What are the costs of Japan's lack of political leadership? Japan's experience in the Persian Gulf War—an issue in which I myself was deeply involved—provides an illustration of some of these costs.

It is an article of faith for me that, in foreign affairs, Japan must adhere to its close alliance with America. It would represent the failure of Japanese policy if America were to reject international society and choose the path of isolationism. From this point of view, the 1990–91 Gulf crisis was a painful lesson for Japan. Our response during the Gulf War disappointed Japan's friends in America and gave new ammunition to Japan's critics. Why did this happen?

When Saddam Hussein occupied Kuwait in August 1990, America's primary concern was the protection of Saudi Arabia. Military experts at the time judged that if Iraq attacked Saudi Arabia, Saddam would gain control of the major Saudi oil fields within two weeks, putting him in command of oil wells in Iraq, Kuwait, and Saudi Arabia—a full 55 percent of the world's oil supply. The world price of oil would then be in the control of an unscrupulous dictator. America's biggest fear was the tremendous blow the world economies would suffer as a result.

Prior to the crisis, policy coordination between Japan and the United States on a range of other issues had been making good progress. America therefore expected Japan to stand with it against Saddam. Japan betrayed that expectation.

Early in the crisis, the U.S. government requested that Japan deploy transport craft to carry military supplies. The Japanese government refused without giving the issue any serious thought, citing constitutional restraints. America then requested supply ships. Japan again said, "No." Next came military tankers. Again, "No." Non-military ships? Here, Japan did at last respond by sending three ships, two Japanese and one American, but by the time they left port at the end of September, the peak demand for transport had passed. America then requested the deployment of mine sweepers to the Gulf. Japan refused. The government did ultimately send mine sweepers, but not until the war had ended. Japan's response came too late; we were unable to cooperate when we were really needed.

The same happened regarding cooperation in airlift efforts. America requested an airlift for the immediate transport of supplies and troops from American bases to the east coast of Saudi Arabia. The Japanese government tried somehow to respond to this request under the rubric of "aid to the Middle East." Even then, the discussion between the Foreign Ministry, Transport Ministry, and Japan Air Lines absorbed long days and nights, and resulted in a convoluted plan. The airline would make three stops between Narita (Tokyo) airport and its final destination, transferring the supplies to different aircraft at each stop. The process would require seven days, and the airline reserved the right to inspect the cargo.

In thus arranging to use Japanese civilian aircraft for military purposes, Japan did make what we could call a real decision, but it did not come in time to meet actual needs. In the end, Japan scrapped the plan and instead called an American airline company and within twenty-four hours concluded a contract to charter more than eighty flights directly to the area. The Japanese government offered the planes for American use. The American military naturally responded with enthusiasm, but how different would have been the international impression if the planes had flown the Japanese flag.

Plans to deploy Self-Defense Force craft to transport refugees were drafted but never carried out. The plan called for SDF aircraft to fly to Egypt, make Cairo their landing base, and travel back and forth to Jordan and Syria to carry refugees from Iraq. The SDF was ordered to make preparations, and the necessary arrangements were made with the Egyptian government. When the moment actually arrived, however, the government could not bring itself to give the green light. It feared domestic criticism for deploying SDF aircraft overseas. In the final analysis, Japan was unable to respond to America's expectations of substantive contributions.

How did Japan fare with capital support?

Some people in Japan charged that a bankrupt America unable to fight its own battles was going to war on Japanese and German money. This is patently false. Financial cooperation was only fourth or fifth among the requests America made of Japan. It was Japan that, unable to deploy even a single person to the Gulf region, instead sought to get by simply by writing checks. Japan chose to become a mere dispenser of cash, and in consequence found itself paying the staggering sum of $9 billion. It is crucial that we not misunderstand how this came about.

There is some confusion about the actual amount Japan offered, but, by any standard, it was an extraordinary amount of money. This is the consequence when a fully sovereign nation is unable to cooperate in international security efforts and tries to limit its own burden to money. Korea and the Philippines deployed troops and received recognition accordingly. But no matter how much money Japan spent, the respect of its partners would not be forthcoming.

After the war, an SDF official had a conversation with an American officer who had actually fought at the front. When the talk turned to the role Japan had played in the war, the SDF officer strongly defended Japan's contribution: "Japan sent no personnel but each citizen gave more than $100 to the effort." His calculation was based on Japan's $13 billion total contribution, including aid given to Gulf region nations. The American officer answered, "Fine, I'll give you $100, and you go and fight in my place." The SDF officer could not reply. I'm repeating the story here second-hand, but it is a clear expression of the decisive difference between personnel and capital contributions.

Since the war, America's definition of "ally" has become the twenty-eight countries that risked their people's lives on the battle-fields of the Gulf War. Naturally, Japan is not counted among them. In a psychological sense, Japan distanced itself from America's image of an ally. As a nation that seeks to preserve its strong alliance with the United States, Japan cannot but acknowledge that we suffered a serious "defeat" in the Persian Gulf War.

The Government as "Corporate Lawyer"

No one would deny that Japan is now counted among the world's great powers. It has repeatedly served on the United Nations Security Council as a non-permanent member and is a member of the Group of Seven (G-7) leading industrialized nations. Japan's power, however, is limited to the economic and the technological.

Our strengths, that is, lie not with the government but with the private sector, because the only function our government is expected to perform is to enable private interests to pursue their profits to the maximum. Japanese citizens expect nothing more of their government than that it play the role of "corporate lawyer."

This tendency will only be aggravated unless the government and bureaucracy learn to behave as impartial regulators. The obvious danger is that the government and bureaucracy become the defenders, advocates, and, in extreme cases, hostages of various special interests. The paramount question that arises is what constitutes the national interest.

Our inability to define the national interest is another principal cause of Japanese political weakness. In the most general terms, the national interest embraces both short-term, specific, tangible aims, and mid- to long-term, general, abstract goals. The artful combination of these two aspects in foreign policy is said to reflect the maturity of a nation. But as long as the Japanese government limits itself to defending private, essentially economic interests, the "national interest" it pursues will invariably be of the short-term variety. It will not be the longer-term national interest that clearly demanded that we strengthen our alliance with America by making contributions of personnel to the Gulf War effort.

With this in mind, it is sobering to imagine what would have happened if Saddam Hussein had not released the hostages, who included some Japanese, as readily as he did. Unquestionably, the vast majority of Japanese citizens would have insisted that the release of the hostages be the government's top priority. The administration would have been forced to try to ransom the Japanese hostages—however dubious the prospects for success—because the Japanese people demand of their government only that it defend their personal interests.

But suppose the government had been overwhelmed by the public outcry, and had been the first country to make moves to free its people. It would have meant relinquishing the vow Japan had made as a member of international society "not to appease Hussein." The international community would have completely lost trust in Japan, and Japan would have found itself isolated. Moreover, though such issues were not given serious consideration at the time, it obviously would have been a great loss to the long-term national interest if the war itself had dragged on, as Japan's economy would have suffered as a result. Despite these realities, our citizens raise their voices only on behalf of short-term, immediate interests. This inability to define the national interest is a serious political weakness.

A third cause of Japan's political weakness is the Japanese psychology itself. The fact is that, deep down, most Japanese want to be able to avoid that troublesome area called "foreign relations." They want to carry on with their peaceful and comfortable lives, and live with their age-old systems, practices, and customs without worries about the future. Simply put, the Japanese people want the luxury of reacting only when absolutely necessary, and want as little participation as possible in international society.

For that reason, when Japan does act in conformity with shared international values and thereby threatens a particular domestic interest, the domestic interest considers itself unduly sacrificed. This is the case with the GATT Uruguay Round. When problems like this arise, we somehow fail to focus on the fact that free trade is vital to the very life of the Japanese economy, and to the healthy development of the international economy as a whole.

Let us bear in mind what it was that enabled Japan to become an "economic superpower." Let us remember that it was the existence of an international community based on the shared values of liberty and democracy that nurtured Japan's growth. We could, of course, in theory choose to return to the insularity of the Edo period (1615–1867) and its narrow, limited possibilities. But if we want to maintain and enhance the prosperity we enjoy today, we must conform to the principles of international society and cooperate in order to bring about worldwide development. That is surely the path along which Japan's national interest lies.

In my view, the "defeat" that Japan suffered in the Gulf War was the direct consequence of our failure to recognize what constitutes our own true national interest. We should not make the same mistake again.

The Politics of Indecision

We should also consider what would have happened even if the Japanese government had been sufficiently aware of its responsibilities to international society and had had the resolution to fulfill them. Would Japan have been able to make satisfactory contributions to the Gulf War effort? Would we have been able to show America that Japan is a reliable ally? I find it highly doubtful—there are simply too many obstacles.

Japan faces five basic stumbling blocks in formulating foreign policy. The first, as mentioned above, is the "corporate lawyer" problem, the expectation that the government act only as advocate for private interests. That is to say, the Japanese government does not have the authority to lead the entire nation. In the major nations of Europe and America, the government is equipped with both the responsibility and the resources, including military might, to guarantee the security of the nation. A certain authority naturally accompanies that role. The Japanese government does not have that authority. In Japan, the role of national security does not constitute an "asset." Military power is, instead, treated as a liability; the public tends to distrust it.

Because the government is expected to serve only private interests, it has little authority available to it when it asks something of the people regarding foreign policy. All it can do is try to "persuade" its citizens, which comes perilously close to pleading with them. This is one more reason why Japan was slow in responding to the Gulf War.

In fact, the only reinforcement for the government's pleas has been pressure from America and Europe, so-called *gaiatsu* or "pressure from outside." Efforts such as the Structural Impediments Initiative have recently been made to reform the domestic system itself, but these improvements are consistently based on *gaiatsu*. Meanwhile, the public's inclination to make "international contributions"—though insufficient—is growing. Here too, however, people have the impression that international pressure is somehow involved, that they are being forced to bear certain costs, that they have no choice but to contribute if they want to protect domestic interests. Nothing is more dangerous than policies that rely on international pressure, but that seems to be the only method currently available to the Japanese government.

The second obstacle to the formation of foreign policy is that Japanese democracy—unlike that of Europe or the United States—comes to life mostly in times of crisis. It is my impression that in America, democracy and the democratic system are at their most vocal and active during everyday life. When an emergency arises, however, responsibility for reacting to it is entrusted to a very small group of people. These people have, of course, been democratically elected, but their decisions about and responses to the emergency are evaluated *after* the fact, not before.

Japan's democracy works in reverse. It is obvious that democracy has not strongly taken root in daily life. But when an emergency arises, "democracy" suddenly comes clamoring, with the media in the lead. Even then, it is a democracy that attaches entirely too much importance to procedural matters. Slogans abound: "Debate it till everyone agrees!" "Say no to a tyranny of the majority!"

The situation is very similar to the aftermath of a burglary: people berate the authorities for not catching the burglar, complain that the police net is "full of holes," and lecture self-righteously about how the police could do a better job. Such behavior is impermissible in a major nation in the realm of foreign affairs; it is an indulgence that amounts to an abdication of international responsibility. During the Gulf War, it effectively handcuffed the government on the issue of personnel cooperation.

What we need is an about-face in our understanding of democracy. Where only domestic interests are concerned, it is a reasonably democratic endeavor to hear a wide array of opinions and to take time to make the necessary adjustments among them. However, in foreign relations—particularly in cases like the Gulf War—the political world must be able to decide and implement its actions from a foreign policy point of view even if it means disregarding purely domestic interests.

The third obstacle is the Diet procedures themselves. They effectively tie the government's hands. Decision-making based on unanimous Diet accord is a pseudo-democratic practice so crippling that even the basic functions of democracy cannot be carried out.

The Diet was intended to make decisions by majority rule, but that principle was based on the assumption that the government would periodically change hands. But because of the LDP's long tenure, unanimous consensus has become a fixed principle sought through negotiation and compromise in the Diet Affairs

Committee. As explained in the previous chapter, the result is that minority parties enjoy disproportionate veto power. The Diet also finds it increasingly difficult to lay down bold policies and to respond to crises such as the Gulf War.

The "Diet Resolution" is a good example of this distortion. Under the separation of power, the legislative branch, in principle, uses legislative procedures to check executive power. The Japanese Diet, however, seeks to completely incapacitate the executive branch by demanding a unanimity that has no constitutional justification whatsoever. A "law" may be rescinded or amended by a majority vote, but a "Diet Resolution" cannot be changed without unanimous agreement. Such unrealistic practices should be abandoned outright.

The fourth problem we need to address is the weak leadership of the *kantei,* or Prime Minister's Official Residence. Crises like the Gulf War invariably force governments to make immediate decisions. But the government cannot make policy without initiative from the prime minister. We need a system in which the *kantei* can deliver its own judgment and expect the various governmental ministries and the party to cooperate. In short, we need a center of political accountability.

Under this arrangement, responsibility would fall entirely on the prime minister. Where a given decision had negative consequences, the prime minister would bear the political responsibility. In Japan, "taking responsibility" all too often means resigning as soon as the results are known. But this is wholly inappropriate. Instead, since executive branch stability is desirable, the prime minister should serve a fixed term of three to four years. At the end of that period, he should be held completely accountable for all decisions made during his term. That is the principle of political accountability at work.

The fifth obstacle is the vertically divided administration, in which each division of the government is specialized and isolated and no overall coordination takes place. The most vital policy area, foreign relations, is at present handled as a bundle of bilateral relationships between Japan and various individual countries. This is a reflection of the public sense that international relations involves nothing more than accumulating bilateral relationships with one foreign nation after another. But the fact is that, no matter how strong the bilateral connection, foreign countries do not exist to serve Japan's interest. We are all members of an international network of nations, and Japan's relationships with individual foreign countries need this global perspective. Though this issue has been addressed many times by a number of people, there are no signs of improvement.

We need to widen our vision to include more than one foreign counterpart at a time; our focus must become multidirectional. For example, if Japan wants America to bring its considerable influence to bear on Russia to break the deadlock on the issue of the Northern Territories (the four islands north of Hokkaidō seized by the Soviet Union in the aftermath of World War II) we must also consider such matters as the current state of relations between America and France, Germany, Britain, et al., and the historical relations between Russia and these nations. If any of these countries requires particular attention, Japan must be able to assess the weaknesses of that country, the strength of Japan's own hand, and the best strategy for achieving accord.

The current vertically divided system cannot meet this need. As we have seen, this was a major reason for the government's belated reaction to the Gulf War, evident even in the single example of aircraft deployment I raised earlier. The Gulf War revealed the myriad frailties of the politics and government of our country. Any effort toward political reform will have to address each of these failings. That is how we may make best use of the lessons of the Gulf War.

Strengthening
the Prime Minister's
Official Residence (*Kantei*)

Introducing an Advisor System

Any political reform policy needs to address a fundamental flaw in our political system: the absence of leadership. Reform must focus on empowering the prime minister to lead the government both in form and in substance. We need to provide the prime minister with a responsive staff capable both of evaluating matters of urgency and of drafting policy with a longer-range vision.

History provides us with several examples of such a system. Just prior to World War II, the Okada administration (1934–36) established a Cabinet Research Bureau to serve the cabinet directly in drafting policy. It was charged with the coordination of ministerial policies. In other words, it was responsible for developing unified national policies that transcended ministerial lines. Three programs were introduced: the "Comprehensive Deliberation System" to ensure discussion among all bureau members; the temporary transfer of fifteen special advisors to the various ministries, including the army and navy; and finally the employment of specialists from the private sector to supplement the official advisors.

This bureau began simply as an appendage of the cabinet, but after the attempted coup on February 26, 1936, its influence surged. Even then it did not provide strong support to the leadership of the prime minister. It instead launched efforts to expand its own jurisdiction, and it eventually became first the Cabinet

Planning Board (*kikakuin*) and later an independent government agency.

More recently, various coordination offices in the Prime Minister's Office (*sorifu*)* were organized into cabinet staff as well. Like the previous Cabinet Research Bureau, the new arrangement was intended to assist the cabinet in policy coordination, but it ended in failure. The new organization never truly functioned as cabinet staff but became just one more weak agency participating in the policy coordination process. Moreover, because of its weakness, it lost whatever coordination powers its separate forerunner offices had once had.

Like the prewar bureau, the cabinet staff attempt failed because it was allowed to become such a large-scale organization that it sought independence from the cabinet. This tendency for governmental organizations to seek independent power is something we have to keep in mind if we do decide to strengthen the cabinet role.

In 1966, the First Provisional Administrative Reform Council (*rinchō*) proposed relocating the Budget Bureau of the Ministry of Finance within the cabinet as a way of putting budget authority firmly in cabinet hands. This idea is still raised at times, but I cannot support it. Not only is the Finance Ministry sure to oppose the change, but the Budget Bureau itself will likely suffer the same fate as the coordination office. In the process it would lose some of its current budget regulation authority. Comprehensive budget coordination, something that Japan manages quite well compared with other nations, would be undermined as a result.

We should therefore remain wary of a reckless expansion of *kantei* functions. We must focus instead on strengthening the prime minister's own advisory network. The following is an outline of proposals for such a system.

The *kantei*'s main problem today is its size: it is much too small and therefore is a highly unstable operation. The staff can barely keep up with the routine tasks, let alone take the time to make future-oriented plans for prime ministerial action. It cannot react with sufficient speed or competence in an emergency.

Furthermore, because the prime minister cannot possibly keep an eye on the entire cabinet, he cannot put the cabinet meetings to constructive use. In other words, the prime minister is simply not in a position to exercise leadership.

Reform means strengthening the posts of prime minister's aide (*hishokan*), chief cabinet secretary, and deputy chief cabinet secretary. They are, effectively, the hands and feet of the prime minister, and he needs a large and diverse group available to him. He also needs specialists as advisors.

Keep the Focus on the Prime Minister

The chief and deputy chief cabinet secretaries and prime minister's aides are today his closest assistants. Their allegiance is to his administration, rather than to particular ministries, and it is they who must be the core of the newly expanded staff.

Consider the following type of reform. The chief cabinet secretary becomes a "chief advisor" (*shuseki hosakan*) in charge of the Cabinet Advisors' Office. Under him, a coordination advisor and an administrative advisor—roughly equivalent to today's two deputy chief cabinet secretaries—are appointed. Also appointed are three additional advisors, one each for planning, security, and communications. The object of replacing the chief cabinet secretary with a prime ministerial advisor is to ensure the prime minister's place at the center of the cabinet, in both form and substance. Marshaling the staff around the prime minister should also enable the *kantei* to operate more flexibly.

The chief advisor would naturally have the rank of a cabinet minister. He would represent the *kantei* position in cabinet deliberations and lead cabinet meetings alongside the prime minister. The chief advisor would also perform the vital role of coordinating the expanded *kantei*.

This coordination role would have to be addressed in the selection of the chief advisor. The kind of role played by the White House chief of staff is probably appropriate. We have already seen powerful politicians appointed to that post, indicating a growing

THE PRIME MINISTER'S OFFICIAL RESIDENCE TODAY

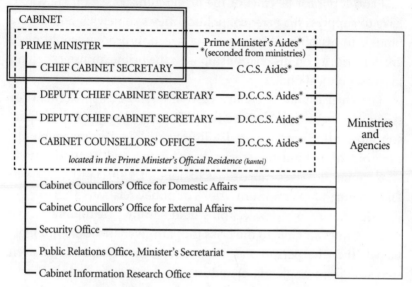

THE PRIME MINISTER'S OFFICIAL RESIDENCE AS PROPOSED HERE

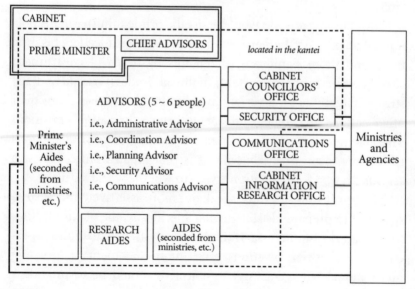

awareness of its importance. The chief advisor, however, would first and foremost be chief of the prime minister's staff. He would have to suppress his personal political views somewhat and devote himself to his office. Moreover, the selection process would place greater priority on his relationship with the prime minister than on his own political rank.

The chief cabinet secretary currently serves as spokesman for the government, but I believe that this must change. A single person, no matter how talented, cannot satisfactorily manage both the role of behind-the-scenes coordinator and that of public spokesman. It makes more sense to appoint a specialist advisor to take command of communications or public relations.

The priority in staff selection would naturally be finding people with qualities suitable to the tasks they are given. It would not matter whether the person was a bureaucrat or a politician or even someone from academia or industry, as long as he had the background and abilities necessary to do the job. But let me emphasize that the person must not be selected simply because it is his turn in the rotation, as has become routine in political and bureaucratic circles.

The planning advisor would assist the prime minister in his policy statements. As the personal qualities of world leaders become more and more significant, statements by heads of government also become more important: political leaders routinely issue strong statements on a variety of subjects. Japan relies more than other nations on cabinet ministers to deliver the nation's position. The statement not only loses impact as a consequence, but also fails to communicate precisely what it is that Japan thinks. This is a serious drawback for a nation trying to win the world's trust.

The prime minister must speak out more assertively and needs a specialist to prepare his statements. Specifically, the planning advisor would do the necessary advance analysis, calculate the repercussions of given positions, and draft statements addressing international emergencies. The objective should be to provide a means of communication between the prime minister and the people, and between the prime minister and the international community. Basically, the post is that of a communications advisor. The lack of such a post is one reason why foreigners often say they don't know what the Japanese prime minister has in mind.

The security advisor, as the title implies, would be the prime minister's foremost advisor on global security issues. Japan's responsibilities in the world will inevitably grow in the wake of the Cold War. At some point, Japan will have to consider the role it will play in United Nations–centered peace-keeping operations. Our responses will have a direct impact on our well-being, because Japan needs a stable and peaceful world environment for the free trade on which it depends. This position will therefore be of paramount importance.

The roles of coordination advisor and administration advisor would be the same as those currently performed by the deputy chief cabinet secretaries, but their relationship with the prime minister would be more direct. They would also share staff with the prime minister. Our goal is to enable them to work more intimately with the prime minister than has previously been possible.

The above descriptions of possible advisory positions are simply examples. All the possibilities would have to be thoroughly reviewed when the reforms are actually implemented. But one point remains clear: the prime minister himself must make the appointments. Some prime ministers will choose bureaucrats, while others will look to the private sector for advisors. Appointments will also differ depending on the policy issues dominant at the time. It is vital that the advisors be chosen by the prime minister.

Developing Comprehensive Coordination

No matter how capable the advisors, they will require expanded support staff. This area also needs reform.

At the top of the reform list is the Cabinet Councillors' Office. For the cabinet meeting to be a place of real discussion, the Councillors' Office must handle the requisite coordination before a bill is presented at the meeting. That would bring substantive coordination processes under the direction of the *kantei*. We should also continue to second councillors from the ministries and agencies and must try to bring in people from the private sector as well. The councillors will have genuine coordination powers, thus encouraging the bureaucracy to field high-level officials in order to safeguard the interests of the ministries and agencies.

The cabinet councillors should be responsible for conducting among themselves the discussions necessary for coordinating policy. The number of councillors participating in any given discussion will therefore differ depending on the subject at hand.

Deliberations should not be conducted behind closed doors. Since discussion is part of overall cabinet planning, the active participation of the prime ministerial advisors should be welcome; in some cases the prime minister himself might attend the discussions, which would serve to highlight their importance.

Thus the Cabinet Councillors' Office would no longer be divided between domestic and foreign affairs. Instead, the entire body would form a Cabinet Coordination Office and conduct discussions of all types. The coordination advisor would bear ultimate responsibility for coordination activities.

Security specialists would also be indispensable to the cabinet in its efforts to respond swiftly and appropriately to international developments. Despite the lessons of the Gulf War, the cabinet continues to take too long to act on similar issues, such as the dispatch of SDF troops to peace-keeping operations in Cambodia and Mozambique. Not only will the trust of the international community diminish as a result of our vacillation, but we will also win little recognition for our cooperation once we provide it. We must upgrade the Security Office in both the quality and the volume of work it can handle.

Likewise, the current Cabinet Information Research Office staff (presently 124, with a budget of ¥1.8 billion / $16 million) must be expanded. We do not need an information-gathering organization on the scale of the American CIA with its sixteen thousand employees. An organization of this size cannot be cost-effective, and it is notoriously difficult to control once established. Japan needs instead to strengthen existing information networks and better manage the inflow of information. We should not set up an independent organization but should manage our smaller agencies more effectively.

The current office, however, is short of both people and funds. The present staff cannot analyze even publicly available information. A more pressing problem is the lack of specialists. For the cabinet to keep control of the Information Research Office, we should continue our practice of seconding personnel from the various ministries, but we must also make provisions for bringing area specialists and experts in other fields on board.

The publicity system, too, must be expanded. Our reforms must ensure that timely and accurate explanations are made of the government's stance on high-level political issues, except those specific to a single ministry. Public relations and public hearings need to be part of a unified effort.

The role of the *kantei* is intimately connected to the leadership of the cabinet and of the prime minister. Hiring and organization must be flexible enough to facilitate the work and needs of the prime minister.

Even the building that houses the prime minister's staff needs an overhaul. It has far too few offices. The rooms are extremely cramped, even without an expanded staff. Communication between offices is inconvenient at best. The current building cannot handle the large volumes of information processing equipment needed. The overworked staff already have to weave their way among the guests and journalists who overflow into the hallways of the official residence. This building houses the nation's highest level of political activities. We need to build a prime minister's residence that fits its needs.

---

* Note the distinction between the "Prime Minister's Official Residence" (*kantei*) and the "Prime Minister's Office" (*sorifu*). The former is the seat of the head of government, like 10 Downing Street and the White House. The Prime Minister's Office is an administrative institution.

Integrating the Ruling Party
and Cabinet

Are Bureaucrats the Decision Makers?

If the prime minister is to exercise true leadership, reforms are needed in a number of areas. The relationship between the ruling party and the government, and the nature of the Diet itself, stand out in particular need of reform.

Under Japan's parliamentary-cabinet system, the majority party or parties organize the cabinet and bear responsibility for governance. Because the legislative majority and the executive branch are comprised of mostly the same people, we would naturally expect them to exercise strong leadership as they work in concert with one another. In reality, however, the confederation itself manages to hamper the leadership of the prime minister. Why is this?

The 1947 constitution recognized that the failure of Japan's prewar path was the result of the excessive dispersion of power. It therefore made the cabinet answerable to the nation's highest authority, the Diet. In short, Japan was to have a parliamentary-cabinet system in the true meaning of the term. The prime minister–led cabinet, it followed, would be very powerful.

The prewar bureaucratic system has, however, remained in place, as has the tendency to believe that true power lies with bureaucrats, who are viewed with great respect and considered superior to politicians. Thus, even when a party holds a majority in the Diet and runs the administration, the impression remains—in the general public as well as in the government—that it lies outside the real organs of government.

The LDP, for example, routinely submits "requests" to "the government." This custom likely arose from the sense that "officials" occupy center stage and that the ruling party stands at the government's periphery. I cannot help but suspect that people are not altogether aware that it is the ruling party, with its Diet majority, that in fact manages the administration. In practice, authority is scattered among the bureaucracies just as it was in the prewar government.

The same discrepancy persists in cabinet meetings. In a parliamentary system, ministers not only represent the finance and trade ministries, but are also cabinet ministers and generalists who take responsibility for national issues. They open cabinet meetings in their capacity as cabinet ministers. All too often, however, they fall back into their roles as representatives of particular ministries, pleading on behalf of the bureaucrats. Comprehensive policy coordination is obviously difficult under such circumstances.

This would not be the case if the prime minister took the lead in the cabinet. It might in fact be preferable in times of rapid change for the prime minister to make decisions on his own responsibility rather than to rely on consultations with the cabinet. As it stands now, however, the prime minister is barely able to oversee ministerial appointments and dismissals, and has no means of assuring his power or exercising leadership. Coordination requires making the rounds in advance to obtain consensus. Any decision thus demands a great deal of time and energy, leaving little time to consider what should be the priority: policy content, coordination with other countries, and communication with the Japanese public. The result is that we are unlikely to be able to take full advantage of a strengthened *kantei* of the sort I am proposing here.

How does Britain, the prototypical parliamentary-cabinet government, handle these issues? The British parliamentary-cabinet system was founded on the principle that ultimate power lies in the publicly elected Parliament. The cabinet, as center of the nation's government, represented the sovereign king and formed a "committee" with Parliament. Executive authority (the king's representative) came from the legislative branch (or Parliament). That is to say, the legislative and executive branches merge in the British cabinet. Authority is concentrated—making strong government possible—while Parliament's check operates to guarantee democratic governance.

Japan has many things to learn from the British system. If Japan pursues political reform to strengthen the leadership of the prime minister, a fundamental element of the reform will have to include this integration of the ruling party and the cabinet.

The government currently consists of two parts: the executive branch and the ruling party. Since each carries out its own policy coordination, the policy process is not only complex but takes far too long. If decision making is handled in two places, the cabinet cannot be held strictly accountable. There is no way of ensuring responsible politics.

Similarly, Diet members drafting policy not only lack staff of their own, they do not take responsibility for specific policies. They rarely have the opportunity to learn much about the policies they are drafting. Meanwhile, they try to exert their influence on the government behind the scenes so that the public cannot help but assume that matters are being manipulated in questionable ways. Surely this is one source for the common criticism that politics is hard to understand.

It is the elected parliament, and the cabinet selected by that parliament, that must take responsibility for politics. This principle is at the very foundation of parliamentary democracy. It is vitally important that we return to this fundamental principle.

Bringing 160 Diet Members into the Government Administration

What, specifically, can we do? We must begin by bringing the ruling party's main posts into the cabinet, and follow this with the formal establishment of the party policy-making offices under the cabinet. The party's core offices would thus be part of the cabinet itself.

In Britain, directors of parliamentary operations or those in charge of specific subjects are typically appointed to cabinet posts. Japan, too, must make the secretary-general—or whoever in the ruling party has charge of parliamentary operations—a cabinet member, so that the cabinet can take full responsibility for presenting a bill before the Diet. The cabinet and ruling party will accordingly be united at the highest levels of government and undertake responsible governance. This integration at the top is not enough to assure the participation of the majority party in cabinet planning. It is also essential that the core of the ruling party be united with the cabinet.

The British government has a number of junior minister posts (non-cabinet ministerships), including those for ministers outside the cabinet, ministers of state, and parliamentary undersecretaries. Their areas of specialty are divided along the lines of the cabinet posts, and they assume responsibility for responding to detailed parliamentary questioning. The point here is that the bureaucrats are not permitted to reply to parliamentary interpellation. Politicians appointed to non-cabinet ministerships therefore organize themselves into teams within the various ministries to study policy and prepare their arguments.

Japan's reforms should include the appointment of 150 to 160 ruling party Diet members to the administration. Each ministry would have two or three parliamentary vice ministers and four to six parliamentary councillors. They would study policy and participate in drafting policy in their various areas of expertise. Thus, even for the planning of policy by ministries and agencies, teams of politicians would, with the assistance and cooperation of the bureaucracy, take the lead and the responsibility for policy formation. Policy making would become the work of "the people" in the true democratic sense.

Bureaucratic posts do not in principle need to be changed. But we must avoid the tendency of politicians and bureaucrats to drift into separate cliques in the policy-making process. Parliamentary vice-ministers might, for example, form groups with their bureaucratic counterparts to exchange views on policy making.

Ruling-party Diet members who are not appointed to administration posts would have plenty of other work to do. Initially, forty
to fifty people would be assigned to work in Diet committees. The
Diet itself would become more active than it is now; its committee
members and chairmen would have greater responsibilities and
would require expanded support staff. In addition—as will be discussed in detail below—parties would become centers for election
activities, placing far greater responsibilities on party staff to direct
party operations, organize election campaigns, and handle public
relations. A considerable number of Diet members would be
assigned to these posts.

As a result, parliamentarians could gain recognition through
their participation in Diet deliberations and eventually work their
way into administration posts.

A Politician-Led Bureaucracy

Cabinet ministers and parliamentary vice-ministers should reply to
Diet interpellation in their specific areas of expertise; bureaucrats
must not be given this role. In a democracy, it is politicians who
have ultimate responsibility for decision making. It is they who
must be called to answer, not bureaucrats. With politicians handling Diet interpellation, they would, by necessity, study policy
more seriously. Bureaucrats would treat their role of assisting
politicians more seriously because issues would be decided on the
basis of their work. The political framework would, at last, begin to
function as it was meant to.

The content of Diet interpellation would likely change as well.
At present, questioning in the Diet is formulaic: those answering
the questions are highly constrained by their relations with the
government ministries. More aggressive debate will be possible
once bureaucrats are replaced by politicians in answering Diet
questions. It should also become easier to make changes in policy
by periodically alternating those responsible for the policies in
question.

Politicians appointed to government ministries and agencies will have a superior opportunity to acquaint themselves fully with policy issues, which will in turn benefit their careers. By acquiring the requisite knowledge and preparing themselves for policy work, they will earn the citizens' trust of both politics and politicians.

These appointments will require that Diet members no longer automatically become ministers when they have been elected a certain number of times. Appointments will have to be based on merit. Elections reflect the trust of a constituency for its representative. This is, however, a separate issue from the position he holds in the central government. Government positions must be earned with expertise in politics and policy. The reforms described here are intended to help develop professionals.

Meanwhile, any opposition party eager to rule should be encouraged to organize its own shadow cabinet. We must study how to establish these as institutions. The ruling party has access to the bureaucracy, but the opposition parties will require considerable staffs of their own in order to develop these alternative policies. The staff would be hired by the Diet and the public would bear the expense. And because transfers of power would at last be a real possibility, the various ministries and agencies would provide the necessary information and resources to the opposition's staff. The opposition parties would become able to develop concrete policies of their own and contribute to a more substantive Diet debate.

Assigning politicians to ministry policy posts and integrating the ruling party and the cabinet will bring at least two significant benefits to the nation.

First, the policy-drafting process would become streamlined. As mentioned above, ruling-party politicians who are not in the cabinet today behave as if they are altogether outside the government. Policy is drafted in two separate channels: the bureaucratic line and the ruling party's Policy Affairs Research Council. Countless adjustments and compromises are made between these two channels, and policy decisions are reached only through a series of complicated steps. The locus of responsibility thus remains ambiguous.

What is more, the policy process seems extremely opaque to outsiders and itself contributes to the public's distrust of the government.

The locus of responsibility would be clarified and the policy process would become more comprehensible if the politicians, who today are only unofficially affiliated with policy areas—the so-called "policy-tribe" (*zoku giin*) Diet members who have strong ties to particular ministries—were instead given public authority, assigned formal positions in those ministries, and instructed to participate in drafting policies. The ministries, meanwhile, would not have to expend so much energy trying to coordinate with those outside the bureaucracy.

Some in the bureaucracy may be confused about the relationship between their work and that of the politicians assigned to their offices. But politicians would not be invading bureaucratic territory. Bureaucrats will remain neutral in the government, providing technocratic assistance to the politicians. This is already the case in prefectural governments.

The second advantage of this arrangement is that Diet members who belong to policy "tribes" need no longer be the target of criticism. "Policy-tribe parliamentarians" need not be a term of disparagement if it refers to politicians who are familiar with special policy areas. In fact it is highly desirable that politicians be specialists in various areas and exert their influence over policy formation. The problem today is that their influence and involvement take place "outside the government" and without formal authority and responsibility.

Cabinet meetings, as well, need responsible politics if they are to have any meaning at all. We will therefore have to abolish the dubious practice of delivering cabinet statements in advance of the meetings themselves. If ministry and agency views have already been completely coordinated before the cabinet meeting takes place, what is the purpose of the meeting? The cabinet meeting should be the site of such coordination.

Frequent discussion among various groupings of ministers

should also be established to address special issues. Smaller groups will sometimes be able to have more efficient and substantive discussions than a full cabinet meeting. The cabinet meeting can thus become the cabinet's supreme decision-making institution, both in name and substance, and serve as the central institution of the ruling party. This will enable the prime minister to exercise the real leadership we need. It is for these reasons that the integration of the ruling party and cabinet is of particular importance.

The Advantages of Creating Small Electoral Districts

A Set of Four Reforms

Postwar Japanese politics has been, fundamentally, quite cozy and undemanding. While Japan concentrated on its own economic development and the distribution of its newly generated wealth, it left the maintenance of international order to the United States. The government had two relatively painless tasks: to hear the views of the opposition and to allocate budget funds as fairly as possible. "Consultation on allotments" accurately sums up the whole of our politics. There is no serious discussion or debate on Japan's future course.

We might draw a picture of the LDP and the opposition, each lounging in a separate bath. The temperature varies a bit from bath to bath, but the water in each feels just right. The parties enjoy casual talk with each other across the room; they bargain, make deals. The atmosphere is easy, the talk lighthearted. Somewhere along the way, though, the bathers forgot the fundamental democratic principle that they must at least occasionally change places. Both the LDP and the opposition prefer to stay in their comfortable tubs rather than get out of the water to change baths and risk catching a cold.

We were only allowed to enjoy this luxury because America bore the burden of world peace and stability. The end of the Cold War means the end of Japan's consensual, deal-making politics.

Remarkably, many politicians want to linger in the comfort of that bath for as long as they can.

This snug postwar structure, in which everyone makes deals with each other and no one bears responsibility for them, will have to be eradicated. Politics will have to be transformed by its very roots if Japan is to respond to the world's changes and build a new foundation for peace and prosperity. The more thorough the destruction of the old structure, the better.

The question is not *whether*, but *how* we should demolish the old order and achieve a transformation of postwar politics. I am convinced that the only effective way to do this is through fundamental reform in three areas: the electoral system, the political contributions system, and the political corruption prevention system. Once electoral reform has been achieved, a fourth reform—election campaign reform—will likely follow as a matter of course.

Electoral system reform must be at the core of any reform that takes place. The present medium-sized constituency is the institution most responsible for sustaining and encouraging the comfortable, mutual dependence between the ruling and opposition parties. Moreover, the multi-seat electoral district system forms the basis of the present laws and regulations on political contributions and election campaigns; it is also at the root of our "money-politics" problems. Any change of rules on contributions or campaigns that is unaccompanied by electoral reform will be nothing more than a diversion designed to placate a public weary of political money scandals. Any reform that does not transform the electoral system itself will not have the backbone needed to change the nature of politics. I emphasize here that electoral reform is not itself the aim; it is merely the means to a broader political reform. We must distinguish between our aims and our means.

It is no exaggeration to say that the Lower House's multi-seat district electoral system has been a means of maintaining what has been a cozy, undemanding structure. The ruling LDP would have no reason to want to change the status quo. What is surprising is that the opposition parties, out of power for over four decades, find the status quo comfortable enough to have lost all ambition of reform.

In the present electoral system, each district throughout the country elects from three to five representatives. Invariably, at least one opposition candidate wins a seat, even if he never appears in public. The reason? There is always some 20 percent of the electorate that is critical of the establishment and votes in opposition to the ruling party, no matter who the candidate. The opposition parties can sit out the election twiddling their thumbs and still count on something approaching 130 seats in the Diet.

Extraordinarily, it is the opposition parties that enjoy the greatest security in this setup. The largest, the Socialist Party, seems convinced that there is no need to go through the struggle of actually campaigning to win an election. The Socialists will never rule, left as they are. What is more, they seem content with that. It makes one wonder why they are a party at all.

It is the multi-seat district system that has so indulged the opposition parties, particularly the Socialists. As a consequence of their weakness, the LDP has been assured of its semi-permanent rule so that it, too, has become immobilized. If we are to break down our sheltered, comfortable politics and build opposition parties that truly seek to rule Japan, we must begin by abolishing the multi-seat district electoral system.

Not only has power remained in the same hands under this system, but every aspect of politics has become entrenched and limited. Governmental politics is increasingly akin to simple administration. It is next to impossible to find what we seek in politics: the dynamic coordination, the emergency responses, and the ability to stay ahead of the curve. Nowhere can we find the vision and imagination we need to cope with the complexities of the post–Cold War world.

Creating a Dynamic Politics

The aim of reform, as I have stressed, is the revitalization of politics. If we can therefore pinpoint the obstacles to dynamism, the

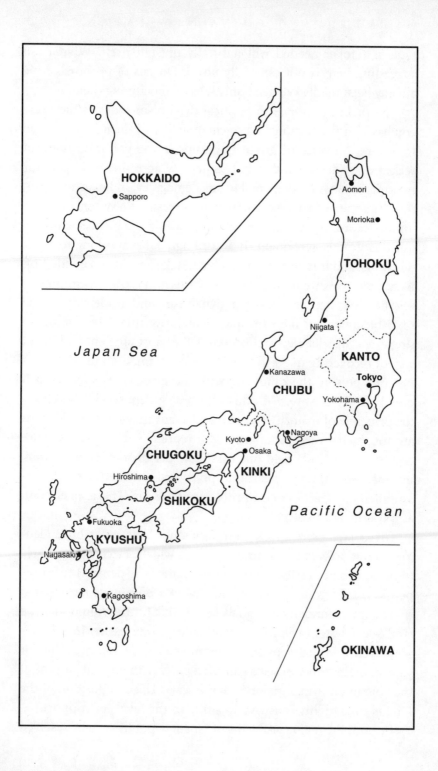

type of reform needed will naturally present itself. What I am suggesting here is not especially novel. Dozens of proposals have already been made. We need only select from among them.

The main hindrance to political dynamism today is the over-emphasis on proportional representation. This principle is designed to ensure the voice of minority groups in the political system; it seeks policy decisions that have minority agreement. Respect for minority views is fundamental to any democracy. In Japan, however, this has gone to such an extreme that the result is a system of unanimous accord. In the current system, nothing can be decided without unanimous agreement. It accordingly takes too long to reach decisions, and it is all but impossible to take any advance action on issues; the pressure to maintain the status quo is overwhelming.

The first step in restoring dynamism and leadership is the reestablishment of the principle of majority rule. I believe that a single-seat district electoral system is the most efficient and direct way of recovering majority rule. In this system, each district elects just one person; the candidate with the most votes wins, even if only by a single vote. No other electoral system so clearly reflects the principle of majority rule. An added advantage is that elections are fought between candidates who represent their parties, since each party can only field one candidate per district. Competition, in other words, revolves around policy: parties are forced to present their approaches to the problems of the day. This is an election as it was meant to be.

Given Japan's relatively homogeneous electorate, whose ideological outlooks tend not to diverge too widely, elections are likely to become battles between two large teams. The demands of competition will mean the emergence of two dominant parties that share similar fundamental goals for Japan's future. Additionally, a single-seat system will make transfers of power easier. In this system, even minimal gaps in the number of votes can mean major gaps in the number of seats gained: a party with only 40 percent of the vote might win a majority of the seats. The composition of the Diet is thus highly sensitive to shifts in the levels of support.

In sum, the major problems of Japanese politics can be resolved with the introduction of the single-seat district electoral system. I am not arguing that the multi-seat district electoral system has no advantages to offer. Nor am I saying that the single-seat system is ideal; it has weaknesses of its own.

The biggest weakness is that many of the votes that go to minority parties are effectively "dead votes." In Britain, for example, the Liberal Party might be in second place according to opinion polls, but it wins very few seats in elections and therefore has no chance of governing.

A second drawback is the polarizing effect that single-seat systems tend to have. In districts where one party enjoys overwhelming strength, opposing parties have virtually no chance of gaining sufficient seats. Eventually, the support bases of the various parties become entrenched, and the standoff between parties polarizes neighboring communities. There is also no guarantee that the single-seat system will result in a two-party system. The worldwide decline of socialism, for example, has rendered the Labour Party's chances in Britain increasingly remote.

We must remember that our aim is not electoral reform in itself. The aim is to fill in the gaps where Japanese politics is lacking. Overall, our best choice is the replacement of the current multi-seat district electoral system with a very different system of smaller districts. Any system built by mortals will have its imperfections. Our effort must be to build systems suitable to their times and to rebuild them when their weaknesses become too serious to ignore. It is an abdication of political responsibility to think in terms of systems that will survive in perpetuity.

We can probably avoid radical changes and ameliorate some of the weaknesses of single-seat systems by including elements of proportional representation. But a simple single-seat district electoral system will be the most effective route if what we are seeking is bold and large-scale political reform. We must keep our focus on the fundamental aims of reform. There will be plenty of room for the specific compromises that will be required for widespread support for the changes.

However, I do not necessarily support a "combined" proportional representation and single-seat district electoral system. The "combination" proposal is essentially a version of proportional representation: it will simply drag the principles that underlie the current multi-seat system into the new system. True, proportional representation does in theory promise that the relative power of parties mirrors the status quo in society. But it does not encourage parties to take the initiative in reorganizing society.

Party organization tends to swell in a proportional representation system; individuals find it difficult to engage aggressively in political activities. We must instead enact reforms that make parties compete on policies, reforms that allow the principle of majority rule to govern politics.

Political Contributions: 120 Million Observers

The system of political funding is also in need of reform. The two basic components of reform should be complete disclosure of political funds and expansion of public support for political activities.

The major problem surrounding political funds is their mystery. Even though the amounts in question are immense, their sources and destinations are unclear. People suspect politicians of lining their own pockets and distorting what should be public policy decisions. Public distrust of politics has so intensified with the recent succession of scandals that it is rocking the very basis of parliamentary democracy, as the unusually low voter turnout rates suggest. Politicians, meanwhile, have no method of proving their own innocence under the current system. Politicians' attempts to vindicate themselves are ineffective in the face of such deep public suspicion.

The best way to increase public trust is to make the flow of money completely transparent. All political fund receipts and expenditures, right down to the last yen, must be reported. With total disclosure, politicians will lose all latitude for cheating, and the people will not have a pretext for distrust. Each politician should be limited to a single funding group, through which all monies for political activities (receipts and expenditures) must pass. These groups will make full annual disclosures of all accounts. This will prevent sloppy mingling of political and private funds, as well as monetary transactions that accompany the policy-making process. For politicians, full disclosure will become a way to prove their innocence.

Some politicians and opinion leaders have suggested that ombudsmen or other supervisory organizations should be established and regulations governing political contributions be strengthened. However, these moves would only expand bureaucratic power—expansion that would run counter to our aims of reform. In any case, we could not have very high expectations of such supervision. Full disclosure, on the other hand, would mean that 120 million people would have their eyes on the flow of political money. This is by far the most democratic and effective method of supervision.

Companies and other groups must not be allowed to give money to individual politicians. They should instead be limited to contributing only to political parties. This may sound strange, but if we are to recover the trust of the people we have to remove all room for doubt about the relationship between individual politicians and companies, unions, or any other group.

On the other hand, if politicians are only allowed to receive funds from individuals, they will not be able to accumulate the money they need. Public funds will therefore have to cover some of the cost of political activities. Whatever the amounts—say ten or twenty million yen a month—they must be enough to pay for political activities. Public money will naturally be deposited with the politician's single funding body and be subject to the same disclosure as any other money. Public funds should also be distributed to the various parties in proportion to the number of seats they hold. The inevitable postal, communications, and transportation costs of political activities can simply be made free of charge.

Public funding is likely to reach up to ¥100 billion annually. If such a system helps restore a healthy democratic politics, however, it will be inexpensive compared to the cost of today's repeated political scandals, political stalemates, and public distrust.

Concurrently with these funding reforms, we should also strengthen the penalties on violators and reinforce the political corruption prevention system. Concretely, this would mean the suspension of the violator's right to vote or run for office. It would also mean bolstering the system to penalize accomplices to prevent violators from conspiring to evade responsibility.

These punishments are of course too harsh if weighed against those for other crimes. But if politicians are serious about responsible governing, they should undertake to govern and regulate themselves with these measures. The politicians themselves should set the example of responsibility and ethical behavior in this system—as in the full-disclosure system—by imposing on themselves the strictest standards.

Policy-Centered, Party-Directed Election Campaigns

How should party candidates be chosen in the small-district system proposed here? If our aim is elections that are fought among parties rather than individuals, the parties themselves should choose the candidates, thereby concentrating power in party headquarters and bolstering party order. But this is risky: power that becomes excessively concentrated in the party executive easily slips into oligarchic control. The party bureaucracy would inevitably become more dominant as well, which might hamper the ability of the parties to attract a wide range of able people.

Given these concerns, the parties' local branches—and not the headquarters—should decide which candidates to field. An alternative to this approach is party primaries, but I am against this method because of a number of possible abuses. One such problem is that party primaries would not be subject to the Laws Governing Elections to Public Office, so that financially strong candidates could spend money without legal limitations. This would minimize the significance of electoral reforms. And, if the law is amended to prevent such abuses, the danger arises that government branches would intervene in party affairs.

A qualifying exam system for candidates, similar to that used by the British Conservative Party, would be most valuable for attracting a diverse and capable group of candidates. Bureaucrats, business people, farmers, merchants, and anyone else who desires to enter politics can take the exam. Those who do not pass the test may not stand for election no matter what their status.

The exam would not limit candidacies to those who score well on written exams. It would instead seek to determine whether a person can effectively conduct election campaigns or handle the responsibilities of a member of parliament. Pertinent characteristics—the abilities to demonstrate good judgment, to argue a point logically and consistently, to speak persuasively before large numbers of people, to exhibit self-assurance in debate—would be ascertained through interviews and mock debates. Those who pass the test would then be registered on the party headquarters roster, from which local party branches could select candidates appropriate to them. Aspiring politicians would accordingly strive to acquire the abilities necessary for policy debates and other political activities. An examination system would also reduce the chances of ill-equipped candidates running for office.

How would local branches be assembled?

In the case of the LDP, the most realistic approach would be to reorganize the personal support groups (*koenkai*) of individual candidates, which have already been developed in each district. Such a reorganization would run into serious resistance. The existing support groups, however, are not motivated by impassioned support of particular politicians. They are simply groups trying to send their chosen representative to the Diet. The presence of so many second-generation Diet members testifies to the priorities of the support groups. The most rational course would be to reorganize such groups into local party branches so that they secure an established place in the system.

If, as I have suggested, local branches are to run the elections and politics is to be centered on the parties, we are going to need new laws that clarify the status of parties. In order to qualify for public funds, groups will have to meet fixed eligibility requirements. These requirements will, of course, be ideologically blind: any group that fields candidates in an election would be equally eligible for funding.

Two other issues remain: election campaigns and public assistance to those campaigns. Campaign-related political broadcasts should be permitted, within the limits of the constitution, only to parties. Likewise, public assistance should be accorded only to parties and not to individual candidates.

The object of the single-seat district electoral system is to turn elections over entirely to the parties, which should be exclusively responsible for election campaigns. Since outright prohibition of individual campaigning violates the constitution, a minimum amount of individual action will have to be recognized. That means that campaign sound trucks and space on official billboards for campaign posters will be permitted not only to parties but to individual candidates as well, with the caveat that parties be allowed at least as much publicity as individual candidates. Moreover, political broadcasts and campaign materials and mailings should be permitted only to party candidates. Public assistance should likewise be accorded only to parties and not to individual candidates.

The result of this approach is that individuals will have to shoulder all campaign costs themselves and will thus be able to campaign only in limited spheres. Effective, sustained campaigns will be possible only in the hands of the parties. Measures such as these are intended to neutralize the campaign advantage of parties and candidates with large private funds and to reduce the number of unaffiliated candidates.

Because only official parties will be able to run effective campaigns, parties will compete with each other based on policies rather than on financial advantage. With elections managed by the parties, the kinds of factional abuses we have seen in the LDP are likely to be corrected in the process.

The Upper House election system must also be thoroughly reformed. It should not mirror the party format of the Lower

House elections if the Upper House is to have an independent function. Upper House elections can represent something other than party allegiances. We need to address what role the Upper House should fulfill.

Unlike the Lower House, the Upper House should represent concerns beyond the local. Under the current constitution, however, it has the same direct election system as the Lower House and roughly similar powers. It appears to have important power in its own right, but in reality it is rarely able to play an independent role. We must keep in mind the distinction between the two Houses as we try to develop an election system appropriate for the Upper House. While the Upper House should undertake reforms of its own accord, the public must also take a more serious and active interest in the possible role of the Upper House.

Diet Members Belong in the Diet

The ills of the Diet itself also need to be diagnosed. I have already discussed how unanimous consensus-building hinders government leadership, but there are a number of other weapons in the Diet process that the opposition parties use to obstruct the government.

Odd as it may seem, the first is the brevity of Diet sessions. The Diet not only has shorter sessions than the legislatures of other major nations, but we also have multiple sessions within a year. They operate on a principle known as "discontinuity," meaning that any bills still under discussion at the end of one session must be reintroduced at the start of the next session. The arguments for the bill are then explained from scratch. It is hard to imagine a system less conducive to the passage of legislation.

To further bottleneck the proceedings, other committees are not permitted to conduct substantive deliberations when the Lower House Budget Committee is in session. Since committees can meet only two days per week, this leaves only ten days or so in a regular Diet session for other standing committees of the Lower House to meet and deliberate. Again, the system seems designed to ensure that as little discussion as possible takes place.

As practiced today, politics is characterized by government or ruling party attempts to pass legislation and opposition party attempts to prevent passage of the same. The system itself becomes a weapon of resistance in the hands of the opposition. The advantage of this system is that it acts as a brake on the ruling party. This is especially important since Japan has not seen a transfer of power in half a century and because the ruling party, as a permanent majority, is almost always able to pass its bills. However, governance becomes immobilized when such obstructions are carried too far. We must reform the Diet processes in conjunction with reforms of the electoral system.

Since concrete proposals for Diet reform have been extensively discussed elsewhere, I will here simply clarify what should be the goals of reform. Greater efficiency is called for in the Diet session. Foreign relations often demand that we quickly and flexibly review various domestic practices. We cannot continue to take months or even years to handle even the most trivial reforms. We will see more progress if the Diet remains in session throughout the year. Diet members belong in the Diet. They must increase the number of days spent in substantive deliberations, and focus on debates over policy. That is, after all, the very nature of the job they were elected to perform.

Second, we must do away with the various irrational customs that have evolved in the Diet. The ban, for example, on the meetings of other standing committees while the Budget Committee is in session is ridiculous. Committees can and should meet concurrently. It is neither reasonable nor practical to require cabinet ministers to attend all Budget Committee meetings. In Chapter 5, I argued that it is politicians such as parliamentary vice-ministers, not bureaucrats, who must respond to Diet questioning, but it is also desirable that ruling and opposition party politicians debate with each other even when cabinet ministers are not in attendance. The Diet, in other words, should become a forum for real debate, not simply the site of formulaic question-and-answer sessions.

Up to now, the opposition parties have unilaterally cross-examined the government, which, in turn, has adhered to a strictly defensive strategy. But the ruling party should also be questioning the opposition. If the ruling party is brought into the cabinet, as I have suggested, real discussion can take place between the ruling and opposition parties. Two-way discussion would deepen the debate and allow valuable views and policies to emerge.

Third, the Diet must become a source of information and education to the people as well as a bully pulpit for the nation's leaders. The Diet is the supreme organ of national authority. Statements made there thus have the greatest formal significance. It is the appropriate place for responsible politicians to make their intents known to the world, to inform the people of party positions on issues, and to raise public consciousness on issues.

Diet deliberations will only become more comprehensible to the average citizen if Diet members themselves fully understand the true objective of the Diet and actively voice their opinions. Parties will communicate their positions more clearly to the people, and the people will communicate theirs in elections. If bills continue to live and die based on deals made in the Diet Affairs Committee, the policy process will remain opaque and the people will become even more cynical and dissatisfied. Our current methods are an invitation to political apathy and have emptied Japan's democracy of its substance.

Government belongs to the people. That is the essential criterion of democracy. If democracy is truly to take root in Japanese society, Diet members must return to the Diet. They must use deliberations on national policy as opportunities for bold appeal to the people, and they must submit themselves to the judgment of the people they serve. These are the underlying reasons for the need for electoral and Diet reform.

CHAPTER SEVEN

Dividing the Nation
into 300 "Municipalities"

Enacting a "Law on the Fundamental Principles of Local Government"

Japan's successful development has taken place under highly centralized control and under the banner of "catching up with and surpassing Europe and America." But now that we have become an economic superpower, we face the need to create new values and a new way of life for ourselves.

Any such effort must begin by encouraging the latent potential and creativity of the people. The most effective means of accomplishing this is by restraining the power of the central government.

In the preceding chapters, we have considered how best to strengthen political leadership. But we cannot undertake such leadership if the government continues to cast its net over any and all issues. So intrusive a government cannot help but suffocate people in their daily lives. It not only prevents creativity from surfacing, but it suppresses people's potential and produces quiescent citizens overly dependent on authority.

Reform of the way the nation is governed must begin by eliminating central government regulation of everyday life. The central government would carry a much lighter load and therefore be free to apply its energies and resources where they really belong: crisis management and fundamental national policy. The increasingly international world we live in already demands that we do this.

Continued failure to do so will put the nation in serious jeopardy.

I am not disavowing the positive aspects of the current administrative system. The system has served us well up until now. I simply want to emphasize that its disadvantages become more pronounced by the day. Times have changed. Whatever brakes there may have been on Tokyo's explosive growth are no longer working. In fact, the entire country has come to look like Tokyo; this in itself ought to be taken as a grave warning. The time has come for what I'll call the "new decentralization."

The new decentralization must reverse the accustomed relationship between central and local governments. Local governments must henceforth take the lead while the central government provides the backup. The center must cease issuing directives for the local governments to obey. It is through competition among local governments that we will see the flowering of diversity in towns, lifestyles, and cultures.

The nation's center has hitherto relied on its own judgment and directed local governments through the dispensation of subsidy monies. Local districts obediently followed along, devised plans that met the requirements of the center, and obtained the money to carry them out. The plans permitted no variance, which meant that local governments had no way to contribute or implement their own original ideas. As a result, every park in the country has the same plaza, the same swings, seesaws, and jungle gyms. Town planning was like cutting cookies: they all came from the same mold.

The question now is how to reverse this situation—how to create a system in which the local governments take the lead and the center provides the support. We can start by enacting a "Law on the Fundamental Principles of Local Government."

The framework thus established would be built on the principle that local areas have the authority and bear the responsibility for all domestic affairs except those that require a unified national policy. Why should we go to the trouble of enacting a law that seems simply common sense? Because, in the absence of such a law, the center at present enjoys unlimited interference in local affairs.

The constitution, the Local Autonomy Law, and the Local Finance Law together form the framework of the current local government system. However, there is no commonly accepted principle governing the division of labor between the national center and the local governments. Every ministry and agency makes its own separate laws regarding public facilities and other matters to regulate that division of labor. Since there are no limits on the legislative authority of the center, the ministries and agencies draft laws on anything that occurs to them. The result is an excessive regulation of local affairs.

Moreover, most of these laws treat prefectural governors and town mayors as the appointed representatives of the national government. The nation controls these local officials by delegating authority to them. The significance of these "delegated functions" is their de facto role: they are, in essence, pipelines to the center. It is through these pipelines—and thus through governors, mayors, and other elected officials— that the central government is able to manage the details of its citizens' lives.

We should also note that central control does not rely exclusively on laws. Subsidy monies, official notices, "guidance," and supervision are all freely used to the same end. The most effective way to change this is through the creation of a law that clearly delineates the roles and responsibilities of the national and local governments—in other words, a "Law on the Fundamental Principles of Local Government." The essential points covered by the law would include:

- The fundamental principles governing the relationship between the national and local governments;
- Work to be managed by the national government;
- The national government's relationship, including legal and advisory aspects, to work handled at the local level;
- A framework in which local governments can communicate with the central government on amendments to

the local government system and on the national
response to local needs;
- The financial demarcations and relationship between
  the central and local governments under the new
  decentralization.

The law aims to reduce the domestic tasks handled by the central government and limit central interference in local affairs. The "delegated functions" would in principle be abolished.

Let Local Governments Handle Local Affairs

The national government needs to lessen its grip on local areas. The most sensible way to accomplish this is with a large shift of staff and funds to local control. All work handled by the local branch offices of the national government should be transferred to local administrations. The national government will of course retain direct responsibility for such national-scale endeavors as public investment in bullet trains, expressways, and airports as well as in police, pensions, public health, and standardized education.

Such reforms will generate a surplus of both personnel and funds in the central government. Local governing units will be able to use their people more efficiently as well, even with their increased workloads. At present, local governments have to assign people to respond to directives and supervision from the national government, but as central involvement is curtailed the liaison work will become superfluous. Local governments will finally be able to use their people in planning for the revitalization of their communities.

Regional governments will need sufficient strength and resources to take on the work previously done by the central government. At this point I would like to propose replacing the current city-town-village system with an approach that divides the nation into roughly three hundred self-governing units. For purposes of discussion I will call these new units "municipalities."

Local government should be a single-tier system based on the municipalities. It may in the future prove useful to group a number of municipalities into something resembling a "province," but a single-tier system is simpler to administer and more accessible to the public.

The creation of three hundred units would mean an enlargement of today's cities, towns, and villages, which are not equipped to handle the new responsibilities they would inherit from the central government. Two guiding aims will help us determine the size and function of the new self-governing municipalities. First, the municipality must have a balance of urban and rural, agricultural and industrial, production and consumption, work and recreational, and workplace and residential areas. The aim is for the municipalities to achieve comprehensive and high-quality coordination among all these zones. The municipality must not, however, be so big that it is unable to integrate these various parts into a unified whole. Second, the municipality must be an area that already forms a community or that has the potential to become a community, both geographically and in the minds of its residents.

Specifically, the municipality will be slightly larger than the 360 "Larger Areas for Municipal Cooperation" we have today (with roughly nine city-town-village units and average populations of 250,000), and much larger than the current city, town, and village units themselves. Needless to say, the mayors and representatives will be elected by municipality residents.

These general guidelines, when actually applied, will not produce municipalities all of the same mold. Tokyo and Osaka, for example, would be utterly unable to cover both urban and rural districts. Administrative issues are likely to vary regionally as well. The framework we establish must be able, in other words, to respond to a variety of needs.

We would therefore do well to establish categories such as "regions comprising core cities and their environs," say, of those containing populations between 100,000 and 500,000. The scale and area of any region would depend upon two factors: the density and relative importance to the area of its core city, and a balance of geographical and regional conditions.

This would be the model for the basic self-governing unit, thereby setting the standard for the powers and resources to be accorded to the units in general. Much of today's national and prefectural authority would be transferred to the municipalities, including authority over city planning, land use, transportation, social welfare, and the environment.

Another category could be "large cities or metropolises," referring to cities that are already listed as "designated cities," or roughly one million in population. Their borders, however, do not need to be redrawn. They will form self-governing units within their current boundaries because they are already sufficient in terms of both scale and diversity.

A Transfer of Both Political Power and Financial Resources

A third category, "satellite cities around metropolises," poses a greater challenge. The so-called satellite-city clusters surrounding major cities contain populations of 50,000 to 300,000; they tend to be "bedroom communities" for the metropolises or to have a high concentration of small and medium-sized companies. They currently suffer from overcrowding because of their rapid increases in population. None of the cities in the cluster has enough draw to constitute a "core city." Residents therefore have only a weak sense of community, and the conflicts of interest between new and old residents have a tendency to escalate.

The basic self-governing unit comprising such areas will need to develop special frameworks to handle the diverse interests of the central city and its environs; the frameworks cannot be developed centrally. Special measures will also be necessary to enable these areas to spend the considerable funds required for them to keep pace with their precipitous growth and urbanization.

Municipalities, due to their size, may not be able to manage the details that are now left to the city-town-village units. Building neighborhood parks, registering residents, or any of the other relatively small affairs intimately linked to the daily lives of residents will require careful planning. It would therefore be best to establish "administrative districts" along the lines of the current "designated cities."

Since the new decentralized system will give special weight to regional ideas, activism on the part of regional residents will be especially important. If the regions are to generate a steady stream of their own ideas for development, the residents will need a greater sense of autonomy and the confidence that they can build their own communities through their own efforts. We must encourage such community activities as care for senior citizens.

Local regions will also need to expand their information-gathering and communications functions if diversity and competition are to flourish in the new decentralized system. Information gathering and encouragement of local knowledge and culture will be among the major responsibilities of the municipalities. For this, they must be able to draw on large numbers of capable people. Every region will need its own growth industries and research centers, abundant publishing and broadcasting facilities, and opportunities for industry, government, and universities. National universities, too, will have to be moved out of the major cities. Financing for this massive transfer of responsibilities will have to come from tax revenues handed over to the local regions.

I earlier stressed that Japan is no longer able to afford the luxury of weak leadership: the times demand strong leadership. Strong leadership does not mean dictatorial or oppressive government. Politics will be charged with building an environment in which the citizens can enjoy maximum freedom, comfort, and creativity. We will only see, for the first time, truly effective leadership when we strengthen the role of the Prime Minister's Official Residence, firmly establish the new decentralization, and transfer substantial national authority and finances to the local governments.

CHAPTER EIGHT

Wasting the Minds of Our Bureaucrats

Building a Crisis Management System

Even if we thoroughly decentralize government operations, the national government will have its hands full with work of vital importance to the nation as a whole. True decentralization would demand that the central bureaucracy broaden its horizons to handle national-scale policy, instead of deciding policy on detailed local issues. We particularly need to strengthen those parts of the national administration that have been ignored in the ever-narrower range of postwar politics.

Japan's bureaucrats have a world-class reputation for their abilities. It is well deserved; they are a true source of pride for the country. But even though the content of the work expected of them has changed with the new political realities, the overall framework in which they work has not. Their situation is the stuff of tragicomedy. No matter how hard they try, they cannot win the appreciation of the people. This is unfortunate for the bureaucrats, but equally unfortunate for Japan's citizens. A paramount issue facing us is the need to introduce reforms both to the work of the national government and to the bureaucratic framework so that we can build an administrative system appropriate to the needs of the twenty-first century.

Crisis management is the most important job of the national government. It is the kind of work the national government should be doing in this era of internationalization and decentralization. Who bears responsibility, for example, in the event that the cabinet is unable to function, through accident or for any other reason? Currently, no provisions are in place. Neither the constitution nor the various administrative laws have formulated a crisis management policy. Our first task, then, is to create the necessary laws and systems for a crisis management framework. The bureaucracy, too, needs to be organized to respond to crises.

The defining nature of "crises" is the impossibility of predicting when or how they will arise. It follows that the best way to develop crisis management is to imagine all kinds of scenarios and begin preparing for them.

The problem of Japan's oil reserves illustrates this principle. We have only ninety days' worth of oil reserves. What will be our course of action if another oil crisis arises? How will we respond to an energy crisis? How will we, a nation that relies on imports for the majority of our food, deal with a crisis in which those food imports are cut off?

During the Gulf War, we tried to charter commercial aircraft to transport refugees and emergency supplies but were unable to do so. We must have systematic means by which the government may call upon commercial transport in an emergency. We need substitute transportation networks immediately available in case roads and railroads are destroyed in natural disasters like earthquakes or floods. How do we expect to protect citizens' lives and economic activity in a major earthquake? Is it wise to have our industrial base so heavily concentrated in a few areas, given our vulnerability to earthquakes? It is vital that we continually strive for better policies.

In 1988, when I was deputy chief cabinet secretary, the military submarine *Nadashio* collided with a fishing vessel and a number of people were killed. At the time, the prime minister and chief cabinet secretary happened to be in the mountains and were unreachable for almost an hour. Likewise, we have no ability to communicate with the prime minister when he is flying overseas to summits and other affairs. We need a system of security, transport, and communications that ensures the accessibility of the prime minister regardless of his physical whereabouts.

Containment of turmoil in the financial system is another priority. How does the government protect depositors from financial instability or the collapse of financial institutions?

Plutonium—particularly its transport—has become a delicate issue because of its use in the manufacture of nuclear weapons. How do we prevent terrorists from stealing the plutonium currently stored in nuclear laboratories?

We must consider other emergencies as well, such as a massive toxic spill into the water supply. How would we communicate with the residents during such a crisis? What is the appropriate response when a dam breaks? Law enforcement and public security include the protection of citizens in such events.

There is no end to the crises we can imagine. Responsibility for responding to them is currently spread across any number of government ministries and agencies. Those agencies concerned should be in constant anticipation of possible emergencies and be continually developing policies to respond to them. We need laws and systems in place that will enable immediate reaction by the prime minister during national emergencies. Today's crisis management—*ex post facto* reaction by individual ministries—is wholly inadequate.

An effective crisis management system needs to address several concerns. First, the locus of responsibility and authority must be clear. If ultimate responsibility lies with the prime minister, we must also clearly designate who is to replace him if he is not available. We must, at the same time, protect against abuses of power. After outlining possible emergencies, we should establish a system that implements emergency measures based on the judgment of the prime minister or his alternates, and that subsequently requests the approval of the cabinet or the Diet. Emergency measures need strict limitations built in to protect against abuse.

Second, training is essential. Crisis management staff must constantly consider possible emergencies and models of resolution in order to train itself sufficiently for the real event. Other staff would also do well to learn the basics of crisis management.

Third, we must build institutions that can keep abreast of, and respond to, situations of potential importance. Again, the *kantei* has to be fully informed at all times of developments in the ministries and agencies in order to communicate effectively with them.

A fourth feature of crisis management is procedure. Emergencies may require implementation of both direct orders and administrative measures that are somewhat different from those of non-crisis times. What is important here is to determine in advance the procedures and the range of emergency measures that can by taken. It is by doing so that we will be able to maintain both social order and human rights.

These areas can be treated under special laws on crisis management. Some people denounce such laws as violations of human rights, but it is far more dangerous to be without laws altogether. Abuses are more likely when emergency powers are not clearly delineated. We should of course ensure that those hurt by emergency measures would later be eligible for compensation.

Without the trust and cooperation of the people, the institutions handling crisis management cannot possibly be effective. This is the foundation of crisis management. It will not succeed if the people do not share a sense of urgency and agree to follow their government's judgment.

Fundamental National Policy

In addition to crisis management, the national government must consider the fundamentals of national policy a top priority.

While local initiative should be given the maximum possible leeway on specific policy issues, the central government will be occupied with larger-scale concerns. It is the national government that must clarify the fundamental direction to be taken by the nation as a whole. Politicians are the ones responsible for carrying out this debate, but the central bureaucracy, too, will have to draft basic proposals as part of the discussion.

In the current political and administrative framework, the central bureaucracies shoulder all responsibilities down to the most detailed tasks. They can barely keep up with the volume of work this approach generates, let alone devote their time to longer-term visions. We need to make better use of their talents: we must call on them to conceive broad policy plans and encourage competition in ideas, thereby enlivening the debate among politicians. It is often said that Japanese do not voice their views. We need to lay the foundations that will help us become more vocal in international affairs.

Equally important are our responsibilities in foreign affairs. International exchanges on the local level are bound to increase, but the central coordination of Japan's responses will only become more important. If we are to respond in a timely manner and from the point of view of the national interest, we need institutions that are free of the burden of the interminable details now weighing down the bureaucracy. Without this burden, communication among ministries and agencies will improve, facilitating policy-making on a national scale.

Security, in all its aspects, is a third major responsibility of national government. We cannot ignore military preparedness as an area of security, but other aspects of security include energy, food, and disaster-relief policies. Today it is difficult to build any kind of comprehensive policy in these areas.

Issues of national scope also include the adoption of uniform weights, measures, and other standards throughout the country. It would be menacing, to say the least, if some regions drove on the left side of the road while others drove on the right. Communications and broadcasting require technical standards. But because even the most picayune matters are so highly regulated, individuals, firms, and local governments are unable to exercise their own autonomy. The question, then, is how much the national government should regulate. Our overriding goal is to maintain order and avoid confusion without constraining freedom of action.

The easiest solution to this problem would probably be to have the national government decide everything down to the smallest details. But I am proposing here a more general, overarching legislation that will require still greater administrative skills. We will also need considerable negotiating skills if uniform standards are sought on an international scale. The coming era will demand even greater abilities of our bureaucrats.

The Revitalization of Central and Local Government

The central government should naturally have jurisdiction over all areas that can be better managed on a national scale. Japan would experience large income gaps, for example, if regions were left to rely solely on local tax revenues for funding. We need a financial coordination system that ensures the assistance of more affluent regions to their less prosperous neighbors. The system should also coordinate the needs of the various regions without infringing on their autonomy.

A pension system is also needed. Early in the next century, just two working people will provide the support for each senior citizen. Social security systems enjoy greater financial stability when handled in larger units.

Large-scale land development projects and public works that require vast sums of money are also national-scale concerns. Highway construction, bullet-train networks, international hub airports, flood control, food-supply systems, energy management, and telecommunications networks all fall into this category.

Working hours and basic education appropriately come under the control of the central government. Cutting-edge research and development in science and technology ought to be supported by the nation as well. Other areas also could be defined as national priorities.

The nation must also shoulder fundamental responsibilities related to law and order. Central control of police forces is a source of concern for some people. But like many areas of government, police activities are becoming increasingly global, especially with the increase of drug and criminal syndicates. The creation of an organization like a Japanese FBI to address problems like these would not be especially effective or even suited to our needs, but the police must be a national organization because the nation is responsible for protecting the lives of its citizens.

There is the danger, however, that a strong police organization can become too muscular and uncontrollable. To keep the brakes on any such development, we need something similar to our present National Public Safety commission. There should be corresponding committees at the regional level so that police activities are always subject to the strictest scrutiny.

Information is another key area that will only become more important. The central bureaucracies have a duty to gather policy information and make it available to the various regions. There is some level of information exchange between the center and regions at present, but the hierarchical quality of the exchange prevents much of the information from being put to good use. We make heavy use of statistics, but we have to be able to gather and analyze more complex information as well.

Information is bound to proliferate under the decentralized system because the various regions will be pursuing their own new initiatives. The central government will likely select the best examples from among them for recommendation to others and advocate new policies based on analysis of newly available information. This process will add tremendous value to their advice.

Up to now, local governments have had one chief concern: that they faithfully carry out central directives. Under a decentralized system in which policies are formulated regionally, unforeseen problems will naturally arise. It is the central government that will work out the adjustments. And since issues will no longer be swept away unilaterally by directive but resolved through persuasion and compromise, we will need that much greater ability in our bureaucrats.

Decentralization and reorganization of the central bureaucracies are part of a single set of changes, the two sides of administrative reform. These reforms are not intended to harass the central bureaucracies. They are intended to make better use of the abilities of the bureaucrats and to set a higher standard for government administration. By transferring the detail work to local areas, we will reduce the workload of the central bureaucracies and give them the margin and incentive to think of larger-scale policy matters. As long as we keep the bureaucrats as busy as they are today, we will never be able to take full advantage of the ability we bring into government. If the bureaucrats have time to study and to think, the nation gains the untold benefits of fresh concepts in government.

With newly defined missions, bureaucrats will also have renewed motivation to work and gain the respect of the people. Regional management of administrative matters and an active national government together will at last present the possibility of a dynamic politics and administration. We will need both for the coming challenges.

BOOK II

BECOMING
A "NORMAL NATION"

Japan's Role and Responsibility

What Is a "Normal Nation"?

A nation, by its very nature, is a selfish entity. It puts its own welfare and interests above all other considerations. It cannot be otherwise, no matter how "borderless" economies become. The reality of the international world is that roughly two hundred nations are struggling day and night for the survival, development, and prosperity of their citizenry.

Nations striving for survival and prosperity do not, however, pursue their interests in disregard of other nations. National security is a precondition of any nation's affluence and stability, and it in turn rests on a peaceful and stable international environment. Since no nation can preserve its economic, military, or political security alone, the world's nations have no choice but to seek security through cooperation.

The Japanese people could in theory choose to return to the days of isolation and to the tradition of finding "beauty in purity and poverty," but realistically speaking, the mission of politics today is to ensure that we maintain and enhance the affluence and stability that we now enjoy. The conditions necessary to accomplish this are peace and stability in the international environment and the free trade that flourishes as a result. Without these, Japan will be unable to survive in the new post–Cold War world.

It is widely acknowledged that resource-poor Japan built its economic might on wealth accumulated in the world free trade system. If Japan loses the ability to trade, it will lose the very source of its prosperity. Free trade itself is doomed without international political and economic stability. Japan must do all it can to maintain global stability, peace, and freedom. More than any other nation, Japan must quickly and actively assume its international responsibilities and help create a new, post–Cold War global structure. Japan, in other words, has no choice but to become a "global state" in the true sense of the term.

The term "international contribution" has been in vogue since the end of the Gulf War. It is a mistake, however, to interpret this term to mean that Japan makes contributions only to serve others, or that Japan is somehow being forced to cooperate with the international community. That presumptuous interpretation can only mean that people have forgotten the true nature of Japan's situation. Contributions may serve international society in useful ways, but they are vital to Japan itself. "International contributions" are essential to Japan's survival.

These observations do not apply only to international security and the maintenance and development of the free trade system. When economic aid from Japan helps other nations become prosperous, Japan's own peace and welfare thrive from the regional stability and economic expansion that result. Japanese assistance in environmental protection not only helps halt environmental destruction in developing countries and contributes to their long-term growth, our assistance also improves Japan's own living environment: the environment knows no borders.

What, then, must Japan do to become a true "global state"? The answer is not especially complicated. Japan must become a "normal nation."

What is a "normal nation"? First, it is a nation that willingly shoulders those responsibilities regarded as natural in the international community. It does not refuse such burdens on account of domestic political difficulties. Nor does it take action unwillingly as a result of "international pressure."

This is especially relevant where national security is concerned. We don't need to return to the Gulf War or PKO bill debates to see how suddenly eloquent we become in self-righteous arguments about the constitution and other laws whenever security issues arise. We look for ways, however fallacious, to avoid a responsible role. The contradiction is clear: how can Japan, which so depends on world peace and stability, seek to exclude a security role from its international contributions? For many people, the thought of Japan playing any sort of role in the security arena conjures up images of a rearmed, militarist Japan. But this is, quite simply, not an issue of militarization or aspirations to military superpower status. It is a question of Japan's responsible behavior in the international community. We need to think rationally about this and develop a system in which Japan can assume appropriate responsibility.

A second requirement of a "normal nation" is that it cooperate fully with other nations in their efforts to build prosperous and stable lives for their people. It must do so on issues that affect all nations, such as environmental preservation. While Japan has made significant progress in this area, we still have a great deal to offer and can lead a worldwide effort toward making our planet more sustainable.

Japan must satisfy these two conditions if it is to go beyond simply creating and distributing domestic wealth and become what the world community recognizes as a "normal nation."

The Costs of Peace and Freedom

Japan is frequently described as a "merchant nation." But when we consider the cost burden that individual nations must bear in international society, it is questionable whether Japan has functioned fully enough be called a "nation" at all. A view from this angle will provide a clear example of what I mean by normality.

One of the best-known merchant nations in world history was the northern Italian city-state of Venice. Even earlier, Phoenician Carthage was also renowned for its mercantile prowess. How did these places fare in history? Venice maintained its prosperity for a full millennium. Even Carthage, which was ultimately destroyed by Rome, endured six hundred years. If Japan, with a little over forty years of relative prosperity as a merchant state, follows these examples, it is conceivable that it has a long future to look forward to. But postwar Japan differs in fundamental ways from Venice and Carthage.

Venice did not survive a thousand years simply because of superior business practices. It was a fully functioning republic: Venetians engaged in politics and security efforts. The Venetian government used skillful diplomacy and occasionally overt naval power to preserve the Mediterranean peace and stability necessary for its trade. The entire populace united to keep the Mediterranean region under Venetian control and was willing to bear the costs of peace and free trade. This is why Venice was able to remain prosperous for so long.

Carthage, on the other hand, offers a rich illustration on how to perish. Like Venice, it too bore the costs of peace and freedom, but it chose a different way: it paid mercenaries to defend it. Carthage was far wealthier than Rome, but it offered no match for Rome's peasant armies. Its belief that wealth alone could sustain a nation ultimately caused its demise.

How much of the cost of maintaining peace and freedom has postwar Japan borne? Hardly any. Yet Japan has reaped the harvest of peace and free world markets more than any other nation. Under ordinary circumstances, nations cannot participate in world trade without pulling their weight. The diligence of the Japanese people, it must be said, contributed enormously to today's prosperity. But the primary foundation of our affluence is a historical circumstance: Japan was not faced with the need to pay the costs of peace and freedom during the Cold War. The world never seriously demanded that we do so.

The threat of communism was what gave rise to these special conditions. For almost half a century the United States regarded Japan as a bulwark against communist might and was content and able to take on Japan's share of the costs of peace and freedom. Had Japan borne these costs, it would not have been able to achieve today's prosperity. We should not forget this.

But with the end of the Cold War and the collapse of the former Soviet Union, America no longer has reason to bear Japan's share of the costs. In this sense, the very foundations of postwar Japan's economic prosperity are beginning to tremble. If Japan evades the costs associated with free trade and stability, world peace and freedom, we run the serious risk of denying ourselves our own peace and prosperity. Despite the gravity of this situation, Japan's political world—which is supposed to recognize harsh realities and steer the country in the right direction—is at present unable to make any effective decisions at all. It does not even fully recognize that we must assume the costs that normal nations share.

This inability to make political decisions means that domestic and foreign politics remain as segregated as ever. It also means that Japan is unable to respond to new and evolving situations. Domestic and foreign affairs naturally differ in both their goals and their methods, and must therefore be handled by separate institutions at the working level. However, they should not exist in total isolation from each other. Our political system must be able to produce final decisions that integrate the two.

Both foreign and domestic affairs must accordingly be based on consistent national principles and doctrines. Foreign policy cannot displace domestic policy altogether, but neither should foreign policy be stalled because of uncomfortable domestic realities. Coordination between the two must be founded on a consistent set of principles.

Now that Japan is a world power, its actions affect not only our neighbors but the entire world. It is often said of Japan that it does not clarify its thinking or the strategic aims of its diplomacy, that it is "faceless" and "opaque." This criticism, heard from both outside and inside Japan, is the result of the poverty of our politics. Contact between people from different nationalities is an utterly common occurrence in today's world, and the world media broadcasts international developments instantaneously. If we continue to act without clarifying the basis of our policies, we risk the serious danger of our real intentions being misunderstood or even deliberately distorted. The failure to explain clearly the fundamentals of our foreign policy—both to the citizens of Japan and to the world—all but invites unilateral attack from those who are ignorant or irresponsible or who have differing agendas. It is not only undemocratic, it is dangerous.

Japan no longer has the luxury the Cold War provided. The poverty of our politics must be remedied and the framework for a "normal nation" put in place. This is the primary objective of the political reforms outlined in Book I.

The "Yoshida Doctrine," Misunderstood

The fundamental philosophy underlying postwar Japan's conservative politics—the so-called Yoshida Doctrine—has been consistently misrepresented. The common interpretation says that Prime Minister Shigeru Yoshida, architect of the postwar Japanese state, achieved success with a political strategy that gave highest priority to economic development. We therefore should not, the argument goes, stray from that path. I find this bewildering.

The decision to pursue a political philosophy that gave priority to the economy, as I explained in Book I, was a strategic choice made by Prime Minister Yoshida when Japan's economy still lay in ruins. "Economy first" was not a product of Yoshida's political philosophy and it certainly was not an immutable principle. Yoshida made this point clear in *Sekai to Nihon* (The World and Japan), published in 1963:

> It was not economically, socially, or intellectually possible for Japan to set about rearming itself ... during my administration. As I think about all that followed, I have come to have many misgivings about the current state of Japanese defense. My view at the time was that we should leave our defense mainly to our American ally, and that

we should put all our effort into recovering our prewar strength and improving the harsh lives of our people. However, both the domestic and international environments have since changed significantly. Economically, we have overcome the need to rely on foreign aid and are even able to assist the world's developing nations. Does it not seem that we are already past the stage when we should be depending on another nation's might in the realm of defense? I have come to think so.

In my frequent travels overseas, and particularly during my recent trips to Europe and America, I have had the opportunity to look at the nations of the free world and to have discussions with their leaders. These countries have already overcome the wounds of war, and I was impressed by the fact that all of them are trying to assume responsibility for contributing to the peace and prosperity of the world as a whole. I have come to the conclusion that Japan too must assume that responsibility and resolve to contribute to the free world.

…Even a Japan that stands in the world's top ranks economically, technically, and scholastically will remain something of a crippled nation if it remains dependent on others for its own defense. It is a position that cannot be respected in international diplomatic circles.

Yoshida wrote these words thirty years ago, and yet they resonate as if they were written today. He offers a clear view of the peculiarity of Cold War–era Japanese politics. But the Cold War has ended. We must overcome our misunderstanding of the Yoshida Doctrine and set forth a new strategy without delay.

Becoming a "normal nation" is not simply a matter of the political world's undertaking its own reform. The Japanese people must acknowledge Japan's position in international society and begin to reform their own consciousness. We must break out of our ingrained ways and become a "normal citizenry" ourselves.

Individual citizens may, for example, conduct grass-roots-level exchanges with people of other nationalities, or perhaps volunteer with non-governmental organizations on behalf of less-privileged people around the world. It is especially important that we, as citizens, grapple with such issues as the global environment, the education of youth, and aging societies.

Japan is fortunate to have the deeply rooted wisdom of a long tradition. We have also come to enjoy vast economic and technological strength. We have to be strict with ourselves—by launching bold changes at home and aspiring continually to new and higher goals—if we hope to be understood and respected in international society. We need to take advantage of our strengths and embark, without fear, on building a new Japan.

Toward a Peace-Building Strategy

Noblesse Oblige

The post–Cold War era marks a change in the kind of dangers the world faces. While the likelihood of world war and global nuclear war has become remote, other threats have arisen: regional disputes, civil wars, terrorism, nuclear proliferation. Confrontations between differing national interests have intensified.

Regional and civil disputes have multiplied since the end of the U.S.–Soviet Cold War. Ethnic conflicts are occurring in places all but forgotten during the Cold War. The civil war in the former Yugoslav Federation is the most prominent example, but in other areas like the independent republics of the post-Soviet CIS, ethnic nationalist feeling has sparked wars of independence waged by minority peoples. Ethnic nationalist sentiment of this sort did not surface during the Cold War; it gave way to the ideological disputes that dominated the period. The Cold War suppressed ethnic nationalism.

Perestroika changed all that. It relaxed the ideological binds and allowed expression of ethnic feelings that had long been stifled in the Soviet Union. The sense of shared ethnicity was the primary force that brought down the Berlin wall and ultimately gave birth to a newly integrated nation. The ideologically communist governments of Eastern Europe were toppled one after another and replaced by administrations with strong nationalist inclinations.

The same nationalism is now fueling the civil wars of the former Yugoslavia and the CIS republics. Ethnic nationalism is the single most important force shaping the international environment today. Sovereign nations are coming apart at the seams: the number of nations in the world has reached nearly 170 and is climbing. The world map is drastically changing.

The "peace dividend" that many were hoping would materialize is clearly not on the horizon, although it remains a long-term possibility. Of course the U.S. and Soviet stockpiles of nuclear arms—enough to destroy the human race many times over, and which, together, sustained a "balance of terror"—will be greatly reduced. The leaders of both nations have agreed to reduce current stockpiles of some ten thousand nuclear warheads each to one-third that level. The United States, Russia, and NATO are at the same time substantially reducing their military expenditures.

Meanwhile, however, the more than one hundred nations of the so-called Third World, such as China and India, are expanding their defense budgets. Not only is there no "peace dividend," but the international situation is, if anything, growing more precarious.

We need to think seriously about how to reverse this trend and encourage a more stable environment if we seek to maintain world peace. A peaceful and stable international environment is indispensable if we are to experience the real blessings of a peace dividend. But the grand design envisioned by America and other countries is at this time still a blank page. The world is likely to continue to witness the turmoil of ethnic nationalism. Conflicting national interests will result in armed confrontations. Only those who go beyond empty words to commit their own blood and sweat to the quest for world peace will have earned a claim on future "peace dividends." Surely this is self-evident.

Many Europeans and Americans subscribe to the concept of *noblesse oblige,* meaning that those with wealth and power have a moral obligation to society. Japan was able to attain economic superpower status because the world was stable and at peace and because Japan was permitted to accumulate wealth though trade.

The time has come for Japan to contribute actively to the maintenance of peace. Even non-nuclear, non-arms-exporting Japan can work for world peace.

Peace Maintenance and Japan–U.S. Cooperation

Our choice of concrete methods of peace maintenance will depend on global developments and, more particularly, on Japan's neighboring environment.

It is often said that the stability of China and the Korean peninsula is the key to the stability and prosperity of the Asia-Pacific region; put another way, we could say that these two regions are the greatest sources of instability in the area. But China and the Korean peninsula impose restraints on Japan in various ways. Even as China seeks Japanese economic cooperation, for example, it insistently warns against any expansion of Japan's political or military role in the Asia-Pacific area and maintains a steady campaign of criticism against Japan in the effort to restrict it. A typical example of this came during Japan's consideration of PKO involvement. China immediately censured the development as a "design for resurgent Japanese militarism."

The bitterness of both North and South Korea over Japan's past colonial domination is still strong, and it continues to prevent the development of normal relations between Japan and the two Koreas. I expect that only efforts over a long period of time will bring resolution to the burdens and legacies of the past.

While Southeast Asia fears domination by China or by China and Japan jointly, its attitude toward Japan alone is different from that of China and the Koreas. Southeast Asia and Oceania supported Japan's deployment of mine sweepers after the Gulf War, and helped dampen Chinese and Korean criticism. That said, we must not forget that these regions suffered severely during the Pacific War and that every country in the region has painful associations with Japan. Japan must be wary in taking unilateral action.

Though its relative economic power has declined in recent years, America remains the world's only military superpower.

The Clinton administration is not altering America's fundamental security policy. The president has said that America will retain the world's greatest military force and military power to fully carry out its mission in the post–Cold War world. President Clinton intends to maintain superior troops and morale; to continue to develop the newest and most advanced offensive and defensive military technology; and to improve the ability of the military to react in emergencies. He also appears to be considering the establishment of a U.N. emergency force that would respond to regional disputes.

It seems likely that America, as it attempts to reduce defense expenditures, will scale down its role as international policeman and lay the groundwork for historic change in the form of a United Nations–centered strategy for peace. Such a strategy would more nearly reflect the reality of post–Cold War international society. Specifically, the United States will probably try to provide a brigade-scale standing reserve army and present proposals to the United Nations for the establishment of a large-scale general headquarters to support U.N. military activities.

This type of emergency force is the kind of institution urged by U.N. Secretary-General Boutros-Ghali in his June 1992 declaration, *An Agenda for Peace.* Emergency deployments would not only respond to urgent regional disputes, but would entail a fundamental structural reform of the United Nations. It would also form part of the American military's long-term strategy. The United States will no doubt reaffirm its resolve to be involved in the management of regional disputes. It will also continue to develop ideas on how to strengthen the collective security role of the United Nations. It will, in other words, be laying the groundwork for the construction of a new United Nations–centered world order.

Given the two above conditions—that Japan's neighbors are still alarmed by any independent action taken by Japan, and that America will be working actively for the maintenance of peace—Japan's path becomes self-evident. The most rational and effective way for Japan to contribute to world peace is by cooperating with America.

The first clause in Japan's *Fundamental Plan for Defense* calls for a U.N.–centered defense policy. In reality, Japan has defended its independence and peace under the framework of the Japan–U.S. Security Treaty. Both countries are committed to the values of liberty and human rights. For this reason as well, our contributions to world peace should be carried out in intimate cooperation with the United States.

The view that the Japan–U.S. Security Treaty has become obsolete with the end of the Cold War is shortsighted and grievously mistaken. The Japan–U.S. Security Treaty is not simply a defense treaty like that of NATO. The history between the two nations is complex. Not long ago we were fighting each other to the death. Our two histories, racial makeups, languages, and cultures could not have been more different. When the fighting ended, however, we bound ourselves together as securely as we could with the rope of the security treaty.

The Japan–U.S. Security Treaty is analogous to a three-story structure. The bottom floor consists of the Japan–U.S. Friendship and Cooperation Treaty, one in a long line of friendship treaties going back to the Japan–U.S. Treaty of Friendship, signed with Commodore Perry in 1854. The full name of the current treaty—Treaty of Mutual Cooperation and Security between Japan and the United States—is an expression of this history.

The second story is the Non-Aggression Treaty. This treaty is, in effect, a vow taken by both nations not to repeat the insanity of the Pacific War. The third story is in some ways comparable to NATO. It includes promises regarding defense, and is the part of the structure that attracts most notice. Those who argue that the Japan–U.S. Security Treaty has become superfluous have only this part in mind.

The three stories were deemed necessary because of the differences of our two cultures and peoples, and because of the bitterness of our war half a century ago. America and Europe share roughly the same racial, cultural, religious, and linguistic characteristics. They need neither friendship treaties nor non-aggression treaties.

Given our history, the Japan–U.S. Security Treaty will not become superfluous anytime soon. The best choice for Japan in the coming years is to make international contributions based on the firm foundation of the Japan–U.S. Security Treaty.

Reorganizing the Self-Defense Forces

We must next consider whether Japan's current security system is adequate for Japan to cooperate with America and to participate actively in building a new international order. During the Cold War, Japan's security policy was in principle centered on the United Nations. Meanwhile, its defense strategy, dubbed "exclusive defense strategy," rested on the Japan–U.S. Security Treaty and focused on preventing or reacting to any direct or indirect invasion of Japan. "Exclusive defense" was actually a policy of passive defense. It was developed within a constitutional interpretation that allowed Japan to maintain its right to independent self-defense, but not the right to collective defense.

Japan's Self-Defense Forces have not functioned as a "military" that independently guarantees the sovereign existence of the state. Only with America's active cooperation under the Japan–U.S. security system did the military have any hope of being effective. This is cold, hard fact. Japan's peace and security are not assured on the independent strength of the SDF.

As I emphasized earlier, however, we must maintain the Japan–U.S. security system and continue our present course in the realm of defense. The character of the SDF, too, should remain unchanged. Nonetheless, as the Cold War era fades, Japan must participate actively in the construction of a new world order. The SDF will be a vital means to achieve that.

As long as Japan maintains the policy of "exclusive defense," the SDF will be seriously limited as a means to the construction of a new order. If the SDF is to play such a role, Japanese strategy and the organizational structure of the SDF will have to be reformed.

American policy is currently leaning toward an expanded United Nations role in the maintenance of peace and stability, particularly in collective security efforts. The key to the reorganization of the SDF lies here. Japan must emphasize the Japan–U.S. relationship and develop an SDF centered on the United Nations. The SDF must become the means by which Japan actively works to create the strategic environment desirable for its peace and stability. We must make the leap from our passive "exclusive defense strategy" to a dynamic "peace-building strategy."

Japan does not have the capability to assume the defense of the nation independently. Our prosperity and even survival will be at risk if the Asia-Pacific region and the world as a whole are not peaceful and stable. We must replace the strategy of "exclusive defense" with one of "peace-building" not only for world peace but for our own national security. The reorganization of the SDF should be based on this principle.

The quality of our defense should no longer be defined simply as "the ability to repel, with our own force, a limited, small-scale invasion." Defense capability will have to embrace a variety of strengths, including those in non-military areas. The SDF must be able not only to respond to purely military threats, but also to take on other activities as well. It must become a knowledge- and technology-intensive organization. We must immediately review whether the arms and equipment currently allowed by our limited defense budget are an efficient choice. We will have to consider what constitutes necessary and cost-effective equipment, and what the future role of the SDF should be, given the responsibility we will assume for fortifying the United Nations' collective security role.

U.N. Secretary-General Boutros-Ghali has urged an expansion of the future role of the United Nations to include not only peace-keeping activities *after* the outbreak of disputes but also peace-building and the prevention of disputes. His concrete proposals include 1) stationing of U.N. personnel prior to the occurrence of disputes, 2) consideration of the establishment of a U.N. reserve composed of personnel from member nations, based on Article 42 of the U.N. Charter, and 3) creation of emergency deployment units that would intervene in disputes in "peace-maintenance" activities such as the supervision of cease-fires. The emergency deployment units would be authorized by the Security Council, and would be under the command of the secretary-general. They would be sent into regions in the event of cease-fire violations or other breakdowns in the peaceful settlement of disputes.

The SDF must be restructured to meet these new needs. The reorganization of existing SDF personnel alone, however, will not be adequate for making the shift in strategy from "exclusive defense" to "peace-building." In its new form, the SDF will take on responsibilities previously not required of it and will therefore require diversity in expertise, including non-military skills, to fulfill its duties. Linguistic expertise, for example, will be necessary as Japan participates in peace-keeping activities throughout the world. We have ample experience in the building of roads, bridges, and communications facilities, but the future SDF will require a wide range of knowledge in fields like industry, distribution, and other civilian needs. We will have to maintain a level of knowledge and technological ability that fulfills the spirit of the expression "a nation's military capability depends on its human resources."

For these and other reasons, we need to begin a comprehensive review of the *National Defense Program Outline*, upon which our policy of exclusive defense is based. The review must be undertaken from the purely military viewpoint of uniformed SDF members who are specialists in military affairs. They will have to give the matter sufficient study to persuade the government to back their plans. This would be true civilian control in action.

It has become customary over the years to define "civilian control" as Defense Agency bureaucratic control over uniformed personnel. SDF personnel themselves seem to have grown accustomed to this definition. The distortion evolved perhaps because Diet debates on defense have so long been removed from reality, treating the SDF as something of an outcast. Politicians bear the blame for having invited the misinterpretation of so important a concept.

The purpose of government is to defend the lives and property of the people. The politicians chosen by the people bear the responsibility for that defense. National security is thus one aspect of politics, and politicians obviously bear responsibility for it. That is what is meant by civilian control. We must therefore use this change in national security strategy as an opportunity to achieve civilian control in its truest sense.

Politics must accordingly take the lead in military issues. The system must ensure that our foremost military specialists—our top uniformed personnel—commit their full assistance and knowledge to politicians, not just to agency bureaucrats. With this system in place, the reorganized SDF will be able to contribute to the building and maintenance of world peace in a meaningful way.

Peace Activities and the Japanese Constitution

It is my view that even under the current constitution, Japan is able to offer the SDF to the United Nations as a reserve force for operations overseas. That is because all such activities would be based on United Nations policy and take place under United Nations command. They would not constitute action taken "as a sovereign right of the nation." Japan's constitution sets forth three main principles: the sovereignty of the people, respect for basic human rights, and pacifism. The preamble further declares that in order to defend world peace and "preserve our security and existence," Japan will cooperate with the nations of the world, and that Japan desires to "occupy an honored place" in international society through its participation in international efforts.

Paragraph 1 of Article 9 states that Japan "aspir[es] sincerely to an international peace based on justice and order." This means that Japan must actively fulfill its responsibilities by cooperating with other nations in the effort to defend justice, order, and peace in international society. What specific means should be taken? The United Nations, as the world's only global institution for peace, is the only possible instrument for this purpose. If Japan offers the SDF to the United Nations for participation in a U.N. reserve force for peace-keeping activities, it will not only be acting within the limits of the preamble and Article 9, it will be giving true life to the ideals expressed therein.

Japanese participation in United Nations peace-keeping activities unmistakably differs in form and substance from the sovereign acts that are forbidden under Article 9. Japanese participation does not involve the use of force overseas based on decisions by the Japanese government and under government commands. This strict distinction between action as a sovereign nation and action under United Nations command is important.

The current constitution does not, however, give us clear guidelines governing Japan's response to international developments. This is why we find ourselves forever mired in arguments about constitutional interpretation. I have two proposals for resolving this debate. The first is that we add a third clause to Article 9 of the constitution.

Article 9 is currently written as follows:

1. Aspiring sincerely to an international peace based on justice and order, the Japanese people forever renounce war as a sovereign right of the nation and the threat or use of force as a means of settling international disputes.

2. In order to accomplish the aim of the preceding paragraph, land, sea, and air forces, as well as other war potential, will never be maintained. The right of belligerency of the state will not be recognized.

A third clause should be something like the following:

3. Paragraph 2 should not be interpreted as prohibiting the maintenance of a Self-Defense Force for peace-building activities; the maintenance of a United Nations reserve force for action under United Nations command when requested; and action by the United Nations reserve force under United Nations command.

Clarification of the character and role of the SDF in this way would help alleviate the worry of those who fear a gradual interpretive erosion of the constitution.

Article 9 clearly prohibits the use of military force abroad by the Japanese government *based on its own decision.* Those who worry about a gradual erosion of constitutional prohibitions suspect that the establishment of a force for deployment abroad in the name of United Nations participation will one day pave the way for Japan's use of the military under its own command. That would clearly be a violation of the constitution. We need a third paragraph in Article 9 to address such fears.

The constitution was not meant to be left untouched, sacred in its original form, through the ages. It sets forth the fundamental rules that enable us to live in happiness and prosperity. The circumstances surrounding Japan change, as do our own needs and desires. It is natural and appropriate that the constitution, too, should change with the times.

My other proposal is simply to leave the constitution as it is and enact a law called the Fundamental Law for Peace and Security. This law would stipulate that Japan, like all sovereign nations of the world, has the right to self-defense; that it will maintain the minimum military self-defense force necessary to this end; that it will actively cooperate in peace-keeping activities as a member of the United Nations; and that it will maintain a United Nations reserve army for this purpose. The Fundamental Law should further include among its aims disarmament and elimination of nuclear weapons, as well as the principle of political control of military force.

Again, cooperation in United Nations peace-keeping activities is not only possible under the present constitution, it is necessary. The constitution does not, however, make specific provisions for such activities as PKO deployments because peace-keeping operations did not exist when it was promulgated. I am suggesting that we fill those gaps with a Fundamental Law such as I have described. By doing so we can correct the misconception that Japan is emasculating constitutional prohibitions in order to become a military superpower. We also have the opportunity to demonstrate the potential for the pacifism of a new age.

People often speak of "wars of aggression" or "just wars." What constitutes "aggression" or "justice"? As the expression "victor's justice" suggests, these terms are extremely ambiguous, abstract, and subjective. It is obviously a mistake to evaluate the actions that people take during wartime in terms of these categories. We must not, in other words, allow a war to be called "just," even if 99 percent of a given population believes it to be.

The only overseas uses of force that we can permit our nation are peace-keeping activities that take place under the flag of the United Nations, whose authority has the sanction of the majority of the nations of the world. That is the principle set forth in the Japanese constitution, and it is the principle on which the survival of our nation depends.

U.N.–Centrism

Founders of a New Age

No nation today can hope to defend the security and prosperity of its people entirely on its own strength. No nation can hope to remove itself entirely from the chaos of the outside world. Nor, as the Gulf War revealed, can any one nation alone resolve the turmoil afflicting international society. International security and prosperity, then, are dependent on the cooperation of the world's nations. No single nation can attain its own security and prosperity without a stable and flourishing international environment.

The end of the Cold War has destabilized the world in many ways. We face conditions of crisis. If we fail to overcome the crises immediately before us, not only will we have to forego any "peace dividend," but yesterday's burdens will seem manageable in comparison to the challenges that lie ahead.

We must consider the central role the United Nations can play in reinforcing world efforts to build a new order. The United Nations during the Cold War served as a stage for the power struggle between the United States and the Soviet Union. The veto power wielded by one or the other of the superpowers crippled any peace maintenance policy undertaken by the United Nations. The United Nations thus never succeeded in overcoming the standoff between the two great camps, East and West.

The situation changed abruptly with the collapse of the Soviet

Union. The end of the ideological battle that dominated the Cold War era has woken the United Nations out of its long winter hibernation. The veto power employed so readily by the two countries is no longer used. Russia, which succeeded the USSR in the Security Council, is still in chaos at home. China, while still maintaining its communist underpinnings, is generally choosing the path of cooperation with the West. We are no longer subject to the confrontation of the two great ideologies. The United Nations therefore is called upon to determine the security policies necessary for today's world.

For the first time since the founding of the United Nations in 1945, it has become possible to lay the groundwork for a security edifice in international politics. It is incumbent upon Japan, more than any other nation, to pursue that possibility. That effort itself is a necessary condition for Japan to live in the world of the future.

The international agreement for Cambodian peace is a good illustration of the United Nations' new role. The agreement, signed on October 23, 1991, by the eighteen nations of the U.N. Security Council, including its five permanent members, and by Cambodia's four disputing parties, was possible because of the aggressive efforts of the United Nations and the countries of the Association of Southeast Asian Nations (ASEAN).

The agreement stipulates that UNTAC (United Nations Transitional Authority in Cambodia) directly oversee Cambodia's administration in foreign affairs, defense, finance, internal security, and information. This marks the first time the United Nations has led or directed the internal administrative organs of an individual country, even as part of a peace-keeping mission. This represents a major turning point in the history of the United Nations.

A Japanese national was selected to lead UNTAC. His appointment is an example of the contributions Japan will henceforth be able to make to United Nations activities, and thereby to international society. It is also an indication of the direction Japan must strive to go in the coming years.

Meanwhile, Japan passed the Peace-Keeping Operations

Cooperation bill on June 15, 1992, and became able, for the first time, to deploy SDF personnel for United Nations cooperation purposes. If Japan sustains its principle of U.N.–centrism, continues its international contributions of personnel, and accumulates experience in this area, I am confident that the day will come when Japan earns the appreciation of the other nations of the world.

We must concentrate hereafter on strengthening the United Nations. Two main strategies will help enhance its powers.

The first is United Nations reform. The United Nations was organized by the victors of World War II to assist in the creation of a postwar world order. It was naturally constructed in ways that suited the interest of the victor nations, as is symbolized most powerfully in their veto rights and permanent-seat status in the Security Council. Ironically, it was these very privileges that paralyzed the United Nations. As the world's nations design a new order for the future, they must review the composition of the current United Nations. Japan should participate actively in this effort.

Second, America, as sole remaining superpower, must actively use the U.N. stage. It must also act in accord with the United Nations. This means that we have to be especially careful that the United States not be driven into an isolationist stance. If America tires of bearing its burden in international society, acts only with its own interests in mind, and thereby weakens the United Nations, Japan's present foreign policy will no longer be applicable and will have to be revamped. Japan, second only to America in economic power, is, of all nations, the one best equipped and most obligated to cooperate with the United States.

America is currently taking a new look at the United Nations. Ideally, America would work with the United Nations on all matters of international importance, and Japan would be able to maintain its two pillars of cooperation with America and U.N.–centrism without risk of contradiction. U.S.–U.N. cooperation would also be the ideal combination for world peace and prosperity.

If we succeed in reforming the United Nations and in encouraging the United States to work actively with it, Japan will help build

the basis for the new world order. We would stand among the
founders of a new age.

U.N. Management of Nuclear Weapons

As we build a new order, we must also implement a concrete peace
policy. Japan is in a unique position to lead the world toward large-
scale nuclear disarmament: it is the only nation in the world to
have suffered an atomic bombing. Fortunately, our national policy
of promoting nuclear disarmament has a much higher chance of
success now that the Cold War has ended.

Policy making regarding nuclear weapons has two stages: reduction of their numbers, and United Nations control of nuclear
stockpiles.

Today, America and the former Soviet republics (especially
Russia) hold roughly ten thousand strategic nuclear warheads each.
Even if the January 1993 START II treaty's reduction of nuclear
weapons is fully implemented, some three thousand to thirty-five
hundred warheads will remain in the United States and Russia at
the beginning of the twenty-first century, enough to annihilate the
people of both nations many times over. Each superpower will
continue to hold excess nuclear weapons, despite their reductions.

The stockpiles are so large because American and Soviet strategies have called for the capability to destroy each other's missile
silos and command centers. These targets are tiny: an ICBM silo is
only a few meters in diameter. To increase the odds of hitting so
small a target, each side must drop a large number of warheads.
The typical example of this strategy is the Russian SS18 ICBM, with
its ten warheads per missile. America has repeatedly called for the
destruction of the SS18.

The quantity of nuclear warheads held by each nation is a function of nuclear strategy. If America and Russia returned to the
1950s strategy of attacking each other's cities, the number of
nuclear warheads of both could be reduced to fewer than one thousand. Given the progress made by the two nations in achieving
amicable relations, a strategy that holds cities hostage may seem

anachronistic. It may be unavoidable, however, as a transitional stage in which nuclear-weapon stockpiles could be reduced before they are ultimately eliminated altogether.

Even if the world declared an end to nuclear weapons, the costs of their destruction would be enormous. The livelihood of the people working on them would have to be considered, as would the conversion of related industries to peacetime industries. The destruction of nuclear weapons will not be a quick and easy process. Japan can offer assistance and cooperation to encourage large-scale nuclear disarmament, and should be aggressive in doing so.

The second stage in nuclear disarmament is to put nuclear arms under U.N. control. This idea is not as unrealistic as it may appear: the heavy burden of maintaining these expensive weapons could certainly outweigh the benefit of having them. If nuclear disarmament between America and Russia makes significant progress and they return to the strategy of holding each other's cities hostage, it will be obvious that their approach is completely out of sync with actual relations between the two countries. There would be almost no remaining value in keeping nuclear weapons. The United Nations would at last have an opportunity to gain control of nuclear weapons.

"Control" or "management" does not imply that the United Nations would collect all nuclear weapons in some special place under one key. The weapons themselves would remain where they are, but all their command and control facilities would be removed from sovereign national governments and defense establishments and put under U.N. control. Some number of troops from nations with nuclear capability would likewise be shifted from their national militaries to forces under U.N. command and be supported financially and technically by the United Nations.

This would enable the United Nations to extend the nuclear umbrella over all its member nations and, at the same time, to check any single nation's effort to develop nuclear weapons covertly. U.N. control is the best system for the prevention of nuclear proliferation. Today's system—the *de facto* recognition that certain nations but not others "legitimately" hold nuclear weapons—is patently unjust. There is ample reason to fear that this system actually invites an increase in the number of nuclear nations.

Another policy vital to maintaining peace is the imposition of restrictions on the arms business. In 1992 the United Nations organized a registration system for the export and import of conventional weapons, but it has not yet functioned effectively.

Japan needs to take the lead in making the international arms trade more transparent. We should issue warnings on arms transactions—which are notoriously opaque and hard to track—that are likely to fuel international disputes. We should also join other nations in increasing the pressure on nations that export or import arms. Before Iraq suddenly invaded Kuwait, it was importing arms of a quality and volume well beyond the requirements of its own self-defense. This is not an argument for prohibiting all trade in arms: developing nations without a domestic arms industry will likely require some degree of arms imports for their internal and border security.

International pressure is sometimes required against arms-exporting nations as well. When nations sell arms in a way that suddenly and significantly alters the military balance in a given region, or when the export of massive amounts of arms to powers that oppose another government takes place, prohibitive measures may be necessary. International pressure may take the form of limiting Official Development Assistance (ODA) or restricting trade. Fortunately, Japan's hands are not sullied by the arms business. Japan is thus especially suited to spearheading such restrictive measures.

In May 1991 the five permanent members of the Security Council developed guidelines for the export of weapons of mass destruction and related technologies. There has been no agreement on implementation of the plan as yet. Japan should therefore work actively with other nations to establish a system whereby nations will report such sales to the United Nations. It must also help establish an international supervisory system to govern the sale of high technology by nations such as Japan and Germany.

We must, in other words, promote policies that will make it difficult to embark on regional disputes and wars, that will prevent specific disputes where possible, and that will resolve them where they have arisen. The PKO Cooperation Law that passed Japan's Lower House in June 1992 opened the way for Japan to actively fulfill its role in building peace.

Establishing a U.N. Reserve Army

The PKO Cooperation Law was the first step toward Japan's participation in U.N. peace-keeping activities. The next step should be the creation of a standing U.N. reserve army.

There is only one reason for Japan to participate in military activities overseas: to cooperate in U.N. peace-maintenance activities. As long as Japan acts within those limits, it will not violate Article 9 of the constitution. To the contrary, active Japanese participation in U.N. activities will fulfill the spirit of the constitution. As I have already explained, the SDF's operations as a U.N. reserve army for deployment in response to U.N. requests and under U.N. command would in no way violate the Japanese constitution: the SDF would not be commanded by Japan but by the United Nations.

History remains an obstacle. The Japanese people continue to have an aversion to SDF participation in overseas military activities. We cannot disregard this "allergy," regardless of whether such action violates the constitution. Asian nations, too, still have an emotional resistance to the idea of Japanese participation in U.N. military activities, even if the intensity of the feeling has subsided considerably in many countries.

We risk, in other words, inviting doubts and misunderstandings both at home and abroad. If we arouse these concerns it will mean that our efforts have only had adverse effects, the opposite of their intended results. It will also mean that the contributions of our young people, whose sense of mission inspired them to serve in international society, were in vain. We must make no such errors in our planning of overseas cooperation missions. We need to show beyond the shadow of a doubt, not with words but with actions, that Japan is acting only out of a wish for world peace. For these reasons it would probably be best—and most realistic for the foreseeable future—to organize a U.N. reserve army separate from the SDF.

We must not deploy troops, as we are doing today, on any basis other than internationally recognized principles. The current PKO law, for example, seeks to assure that the SDF will not be drawn into military confrontations by stipulating that if the cease-fire agreement breaks down, Japanese units will be able unilaterally to suspend their activities and withdraw from the site. The law clearly seeks special treatment for Japan. U.N. regulations stipulate that the right of command over the troops deployed under UNTAC belongs to the U.N. secretary-general. But in the text of the PKO law, the English word "command" is translated into two parts: the secretary-general has the right only to give orders, while the Japanese government retains the right of "command." The prime minister used this distinction in explaining the government's interpretation of the law to the Diet. Thus if the Japanese government judges that Japanese troops are about to get drawn into combat, it can withdraw the troops on its own authority, without the approval of the secretary-general.

This interpretation not only complicates the situation but brings up other serious problems as well. First, troops in the field face greater difficulty because of the confusion in the chain of command. Second, this interpretation is almost certain to violate Article 9. To claim, as the Miyazawa government does, that the Japanese government has the right of command over the troops it has deployed overseas is to say that the government of Japan has responsibility for the actions of its troops overseas. This is the same as saying that Japan deployed its troops abroad as a right of a sovereign nation. It is precisely the sovereign use of force by Japan that

Article 9 prohibits. If the troops we deploy get enveloped in fighting, they will find themselves taking the kind of action that is explicitly prohibited by the constitution. The way we deploy troops today leaves potential for constitutional violations.

This would not be the case if the troops came entirely under the command of the United Nations. They must not be the responsibility of the Japanese government. In this way, even if Japanese troops do get caught in fighting, they will respond not at the direction of the government of Japan but clearly as participants in the peace-keeping functions of the United Nations.

It is time that Japan recognizes that it is an important participant in this new age in international society. We have to face the demands of the new age head on and plan the best course of action. We must not assume that we can evade the responsibility for any mistakes we make, or that we can disguise them in any way.

Maintenance of a U.N. reserve force distinct from the SDF does have budgetary and management disadvantages. However, we should regard these burdens as the cost of publicizing to the entire world that Japan engages in military acts overseas only in cooperation with U.N. peace-keeping activities.

Steering the World Away from the Trap of Protectionism

Aggressively Opening Our Own Markets

The postwar Pax Americana global free trade system is today seriously at risk. "Managed trade" is increasingly common, although it continues to be labeled "free trade" in its many guises. "Voluntary" export restraints in textiles, steel, and automobiles, for example, may violate GATT principles. Ironically, the end of the Cold War has aggravated this risk, as nations focus increasingly on their economic interests. Had the Cold War continued, the Uruguay Round would probably have come to a successful conclusion much sooner, as the common fear of the Soviet Union helped bind the Western bloc.

We must realize that it is Japan that will be most blamed for destroying the free trade system. Americans seem more and more inclined to believe that, although they emerged as "victors" of the Cold War, they face a new threat from Japan. Even U.S. government publications like *Defense Report* and *National Security Strategy* list Japan as the most significant non-military threat to American national interests.

It is already being said that the major failure of the GATT was its inability to open Japan's markets. According to the OECD, Japan's 1992 current account surplus stood at $120 billion, while the deficits of America and Germany were $56 billion and $26 billion, respectively. Excluding France (which showed a surplus of $1 billion), the total deficit of the other five members of the G-7 came to $150 billion, leaving the impression that Japan is "the only victor" in world trade.

This image, along with Japan's burgeoning surplus, shows no signs of changing anytime soon. This is why others claim that Japan is a free rider in the GATT, making little or no effort to dismantle its non-tariff and other invisible barriers to trade. Although Japan has reduced its import tariffs and quotas, its proportion of imports of manufactured goods remains unimproved.

How will it be in the future? The "Super 301" clause of the 1988 Omnibus Trade Act suggested that America's attacks on Japan will become more pronounced. Super 301 was a unilateral, confrontational measure stipulating that if America determined that Japan unfairly discriminated against certain imports, America would push it to open those markets. The law also stated that the American government, acting unilaterally, would take retaliatory measures if Japan failed to respond.

A look back at our experience thus far shows that Japan changed a number of its policies as a result of negotiations with America. Voluntary export restraints are one example. Through the Japan–U.S. Yen-Dollar Committee, America pushed Japan to open and liberalize its financial markets; foreign banks were thus enabled to enter Japan's trust business. Japanese policies in many sectors, including telecommunications, airlines, transport, and health, were altered as a result of the Market-Oriented, Sector-Specific (MOSS) talks held from 1985 on. During the Structural Impediments Initiative (SII) talks, America pointed out the closed nature of the Japanese distribution system, and the result was an amendment of the Large-Scale Retail Law. Many of America's demands for market opening were advantageous for Japanese consumer interests. With the help of American pressure, Japan was willing to reform its domestic systems.

Deregulation of this kind, based as it is on trade friction, is dangerous. America has gained the impression that Japan makes concessions only if enormous pressure is applied. Japan is also frustrated at the thought that increased *gaiatsu* (external pressure) will result in only more concessions. This has spurred an emotional confrontation that threatens to aggravate U.S.–Japan trade friction.

Japan needs a new economic diplomacy. It has to take the initiative in opening its domestic market and fully realize the principle of non-discrimination at home and abroad.

It is not only foreign producers and representatives of other governments who claim that Japanese markets are closed. The Japanese consumer, too, faces interests that became entrenched during our rapid-growth era and that are often opposed to consumer welfare. As part of economic reform toward opening our markets, we must undertake a thoroughgoing review of every sector from the perspective of the consumer. However, where we can prove that American demands of Japan are not rational, we should immediately appeal to the GATT. By limiting our appeal to the product in question, Japan can clearly communicate its intentions to America and the world. An international approach to trade disputes benefits not only long-term cooperative relations between the two nations but the wider world order itself.

Transparency and openness are also being demanded of Japan's *keiretsu*, or corporate groupings. *Keiretsu* have many strengths, including the long-term relations of trust they encourage among related companies. The *keiretsu*'s role in improving quality and developing new products has been widely praised even in America and Europe. But the *keiretsu* system requires modification if companies are to end their discriminatory practices. It might be possible, for example, to replace the principle of non-admission of new participants in *keiretsu* with a provisional "10 percent system" that would recognize the unconditional new entry of foreign firms into 10 percent of *keiretsu* transactions annually.

Along with managed trade, regional trade systems pose a threat to free trade today. The market integration of the European Community in the mid-1980s marked the beginning of the spread of regional trade systems. The European economic sphere is already expanding: Hungary, Poland, and the Czech Republic are attempting to conclude "association agreements" with the EC. America, Canada, and Mexico have meanwhile officially concluded the North American Free Trade Agreement (NAFTA). Brazil, Argentina, Uruguay, and Paraguay have agreed to create a South American Common Market (MERCOSUR).

Regionalism in this form is not equivalent to the pre–World War II economic blocs, but it is reminiscent because it is a means of deepening the interdependence among economies within a region and achieving economies of scale. The common threat binding the West during the Cold War no longer exists, and nations are beginning to act in terms of their own national interests.

Creating a "World Trade Organization"

Just after World War II, America called for the creation of an "International Trade Organization" (ITO) in the United Nations and gathered the signatures of fifty-three member nations in support of the proposal. The idea arose because of the recognition that protectionism and bloc economies had been a major cause of the war. The ITO was essentially a trade version of the role played by the International Monetary Fund (IMF) in international currency stabilization.

Unlike the IMF, the ITO never came into being. The American Congress rejected it because it would hinder industrial protection. Thus the GATT—which was originally intended to be a subsidiary organization under the ITO—has endured almost half a century without adequate supervisory power to enforce international trading rules. Free trade nevertheless survived, albeit with some distortions, in large part because of the memory of the war and because of the Cold War that demanded strong allegiance among Western allies.

Today, however, the relative decline in America's economic status, Europe's failure to make structural adjustments to global economic change, and extreme trade imbalances have given rise to unilateral restrictive trade measures, bilateralism, and regionalism.

It is conceivable that the GATT will increasingly be circumvented or shorn of its limited powers. The greatest threat is the tendency of various countries to determine for themselves the fairness or propriety of the trade practices of other nations. America and the EC unilaterally impose sanctions based on their own standards.

It has accordingly become difficult to predict the future of trade rules, and that uncertainty threatens the world's economic dynamism. If nations continue to evaluate market structures without international standards, they will increasingly fall back on measurable import and export "results" as the basis for evaluation. They will rely, that is, on managed trade and protectionism, which will in turn exacerbate the economic confrontations among the major economies of the world.

Today's global economy needs exactly the kind of international trade organization that America proposed nearly fifty years ago. For purposes of this discussion I'll call this organization the World Trade Organization (WTO). Japan, as the greatest beneficiary of the GATT, should work hard to promote the establishment of the WTO and cast off its epithet of "GATT free rider."

The WTO should have at least three characteristics. First, it should expand the rules governing international trade sectors not currently regulated under the GATT. This would, for example, entail strengthening the Multilateral Trade Organization (MTO), currently under discussion in the Uruguay Round, which seeks to establish international definitions of dumping, standards for measuring local content, and rules governing intellectual property. Second, the WTO must be organized in such a way that the structural characteristics of various economies that give rise to international trade friction are eventually abolished. Measures that are unwittingly discriminatory remain in all nations, the legacies of their various histories and traditions. Non-transparent systems, such as Japan's *dango* (collusive practices), must be reformed. The WTO would also make the necessary adjustments among such structures and build frameworks to guarantee free competition.

Third, the WTO has to take North-South issues into account.

Developed countries have long made the claim that "trade is better than aid," but developing countries continue to struggle with poverty and stagnation. If they are to embrace international trade rules as developed nations do, they must be enabled to develop import-substitution industries and to export their products. Japan and other successful nations in Asia provide many examples of the importance of this process.

Japan has enjoyed the many benefits of free world trade; it must now take the initiative and actively promote the creation of a world trade organization. Japan will only be in a weaker position if we wait until the world has committed itself to regionalism. It will be too late.

These are not simple issues. They are enmeshed with domestic interests regarding industrial protection and are therefore politically difficult. But that is precisely the value of creating a world trade organization with high ideals. As the world's greatest beneficiary of free trade, Japan has a duty to take this stand on behalf of free trade.

Today's market economies can be divided into two types: the free market economies characteristic of Europe and America, and the development-oriented market economies typical in Asia. The latter boast the highest growth rates. Japan stands somewhere in between. It began as a developmental market economy, but now increasingly resembles the American-European type. Japan is in a unique position to close the gap between the two.

Japan must begin to fulfill that role by opening its domestic market to the outside world and significantly reducing government interference in business. By working toward a classically liberal market economy, we can slow the move by Europe and America toward regionalism and prevent Asia from moving in the same direction. Japan would gain a greater voice in world trade as a result and be in a stronger position to promote the creation of a WTO. Japan's response to trade friction has hitherto been passive. We need to become aware that we can and should play a more active role.

CHAPTER FIVE

An Asia-Pacific
Ministerial Conference

An Accurate Recognition of History

Japan is also expected to play a political role in the creation of a stable order in East Asia. As Chinese Communist Party Secretary Jiang Zemin stated on a recent visit to Japan: "The nations of Asia and the world would welcome political, technological, and cultural as well as economic contributions to regional development and world peace by Japan, in its capacity as Asia's most advanced nation."

However, our Asian neighbors continue to feel distrust and alarm about Japan, as a result of World War II. We need to develop the trust of our neighbors if we are to place greater emphasis on our political ties in the region. "History" is not an issue we can avoid.

How are we to approach the history issue? We must reflect soberly on our history, examine it in good faith, and apply its lesson to our principles and behavior, our present actions, and our future plans. We cannot deny the part aggression has played in our history in Asia. The issue is not that we have never discussed the question of our wartime responsibility, but that we did so only at home: we did not face the Asia-Pacific nations we had invaded. We have to admit that our government has not made much effort to settle the past. Nor was public feeling sufficiently harsh to prevent the reemergence of politicians associated with Japan's past aggression. We must be strict with ourselves as we look back on our history, even if we start doing so only today.

We should also be aware that "aggressor" is not the only historical role Japan has played in the region. We also have a history of solidarity with the region, as was evident in Fukuzawa Yukichi's support for reform in Korea, and the support of Inukai Bokudō (Tsuyoshi) and Miyazaki Tōten for Sun Yat-sen's revolutionary movement in China and for Emilio Aguinaldo's campaign for the independence of the Philippines. We must learn about both aspects of our history as we reconsider the nature of our regional diplomacy in order to dissolve the distrust and alarm felt toward Japan in Asia.

Our first step should be to find ways to settle the issues remaining from our past aggression. Second, our diplomacy should strive to achieve the ideals of mutual help that we embraced at one time in our prewar history and again in our postwar economic relations with the region. Finally, we must seek to define Japan's role and responsibility for building a stable regional order through discussions with the various nations of the region. It is precisely this kind of affirmative effort that will earn Japan the trust of the region.

As we seek to fulfill our international responsibilities, the importance of partnerships should be foremost in our minds. Nothing can be realized by our acting entirely on our own. As I have repeatedly stressed, Japan's major diplomatic partner is America, in the Asia-Pacific region as elsewhere in the world. We must also form close cooperative partnerships with the nations of ASEAN and Oceania.

China, the Korean peninsula, and the other nations of East Asia are all important for Japan's stability and prosperity. China, however, retains a different political ideology and, despite one of the highest growth rates in the world, remains a developing nation economically. North Korea is even more unfamiliar, and the Korean peninsula as a whole is likely to be unstable for some time to come as it makes the transition from division to integration.

"Flying-Geese Formation" Development

The end of the Cold War is bringing the era of ideological confrontation to a close. In the present international power structure, military—including nuclear—might is no longer decisive. Nonetheless, new types of security problems are arising.

The dissolution of the Soviet Union will not necessarily bring peace and disarmament to the Asia-Pacific region. Security here has hitherto been maintained by the American military stationed in the region to resist the Soviet threat. It now seems likely that America will significantly reduce its forces in the region, and many countries fear that such a withdrawal will result in a power vacuum.

The fear is justified. India is expanding its navy, North Korea and China are building up their military stockpiles, and some Southeast Asian countries too are strengthening and expanding their military capabilities.

Ethnicity, religion, and territorial disputes also threaten regional security. These issues were largely suppressed during the Cold War, but may pose a serious threat to regional stability in the years to come. Cold War–era problems such as those between China and Taiwan and between North and South Korea, and the instability of Cambodia are to some extent Asia-specific problems.

Ethnic problems are a source of chaos in China, Central Asia, Far-Eastern Russia, Indonesia, Myanmar, and other places. Territorial disputes remain between Japan and Russia over the Kurile Island chain, and between China, Vietnam, and ASEAN countries over the Spratly Islands. The rise of fundamentalist Islam in Malaysia and Indonesia is a source of concern. The confrontational relationship between India and Pakistan is largely due to ethnic and religious clashes. Domestic confusion in China and North Korea is sure to be a new source of unease.

It has become commonplace to hear that the world is shifting its focus from military to economic might. The striking economic development of the Asian Newly Industrializing Economies (NIES) and ASEAN has led a number of commentators to predict the coming "Asia-Pacific century." Assuming that current projections do not change, 6 percent growth is expected in the 1990s in this region, which does not include China, North Korea, Myanmar, and other politically unstable regions. It is said that the economy thirty years hence will be seven or eight times today's size.

The engine driving this development is Japan. Along with America, it supplies the capital and technology that enabled the Asian NIEs and now ASEAN to develop as Japan has, in a process that has been called development in "flying-geese formation." Today, the socialist nations of China, North Korea, and Vietnam are seeking to join the flock. The threats to peace and prosperity in the Asia-Pacific region will be significantly reduced if they do, and Japan must redouble its efforts to maintain and spread this development. Of special importance will be cooperative relations with ASEAN, the center of development today. Improved relations with Oceania, the most advanced area in the wider region, will also be crucial.

At the same time we must be wary of ideas, such as the East Asian Economic Caucus (EAEC), that encourage a drift toward bloc economies. "Flying-geese formation" development has been possible because the South China economic area and the Malaysia-Singapore-Indonesia triangle set their sights beyond national boundaries and on the global market. The EAEC and other bloc ideas will only obstruct development.

International relations within the Asia-Pacific region are more complex than in Europe because the communist element combines with the priority of economic development in China, Vietnam, and North Korea. It is a source of considerable instability.

The demand for political democratization is growing in China, following a decade of reforms. The movement was crushed in the Tiananmen Square incident of June 1989, but it is likely to boil over again if current reform policies continue. But if the democratization movement develops sufficiently to generate domestic chaos—or even disintegration—China's internal confusion will threaten the stability and prosperity of the entire Asia-Pacific region.

North Korea appears stable with its Kim Il Sung personality cult. But it has intensified regional instability by withdrawing from the Nuclear Non-Proliferation Treaty (NPT) and further isolating itself from the world. Vietnamese policies of *doi moi* (economic reform) have steadily gained ground since their inception in 1986. But it is questionable whether the socialist, one-party dictatorship will be able to confine development to the economy when it is closely cooperating with such liberal nations as ASEAN, the NIEs, Japan, and the United States. Democratic movements are likely soon to emerge in the political sphere as well.

Five Guidelines for Japanese Foreign Policy

Given the above conditions, I believe the following five guidelines will best direct our Asia-Pacific diplomacy.

The national interest. Japan must recognize that the fundamental aim of Japanese foreign policy is to maintain our security and prosperity and our role as a major member of the community of advanced democratic nations. Democracy, human rights, and market economics are the principal values Japan shares with other democratic nations. It is by the pursuit of these principles that we ensure our country's stability and prosperity.

Global participation. As one of the world's advanced democratic nations, Japan has a responsibility to cooperate with the U.S. and Europe in building a new and stable order to replace the Cold War structure. Japan has already been asked to cooperate in this effort. Both the Japanese government and the citizens of Japan need to become aware of the nation not only as an economic power but as a political power as well. Political power does not mean imposing our will upon others. To the contrary, it requires that we seriously consider the individual characteristics and special needs of other countries when formulating policy.

Diplomatic objectives. The stronger Japan becomes, the more necessary it is to have a clear, unambiguous foreign policy. The world will be rightly wary of an increasingly powerful Japan that does not spell out its policy aims. Those aims should include the realization of the values we share with other advanced democratic nations, such as the belief in the need for political democratization and free-market economies, and a desire to contribute to the resolution of global problems like AIDS, environmental pollution, and drug abuse. After our diplomatic aims are established, we must demonstrate to ourselves and to the world that we are developing strategies designed to achieve them.

A strengthened U.S.–Japan alliance. We must reaffirm that the U.S.–Japan alliance will remain the cornerstone of our foreign policy, and help the relationship adapt to changes in the international environment. Up until now, Japan has enjoyed the benefits of security and prosperity under the U.S.–Japan security alliance. This system will continue not only to guarantee Japan's own security and prosperity, but also to prevent disputes in the Asia-Pacific region.

The importance of the Asia-Pacific. Japan must continue to give priority to its Asia-Pacific diplomacy. The twin pillars of Japanese diplomacy have been our membership of the Asia-Pacific community and of the community of the advanced democratic nations of the West. The end of the Cold War, however, has stripped the latter approach of its significance, while the remarkable rise of the Asian economies suggests that Japan's ties to the Asia Pacific region can only strengthen. The political democratization currently taking place will further solidify the relationship. It is natural that Japan maintain policy coordination relationships in the U.S.–Japan alliance and the G-7. Now it must construct special relationships of policy coordination with the nations of the Asia-Pacific region.

Japan must do everything possible to foster China's stability and development. At the same time, we need to be prepared to respond to domestic confusion inside China. The Chinese economy has shifted quickly toward an open system and has already been incorporated in the international economic network. China's dependence on the outside world is greater than Japan's, and the Chinese economy cannot return to isolation. However, even as we continue to offer our cooperation, we must take into account the harsh international reaction to the Chinese government's stance on democratization. This issue will require serious and continuing scrutiny. Even as we continue to be sensitive to China's position on Taiwan, we may at some point have to establish some kind of official relationship with Taiwan as well.

Japan has an important role to play in resolving disputes in the Asia-Pacific region. We have already taken the initiative to help resolve the Cambodian dispute. We must also, in cooperation with the nations of ASEAN and Oceania, take steps toward active assistance in the postwar reconstruction of Vietnam and Indochina. On the Korean peninsula, we must maintain our close relations with South Korea. We must also advance normalization of relations with North Korea and help create an environment that will encourage the peaceful reunification of the two Koreas.

If Japan is to represent the interests of the Asia-Pacific region in the international arena and act as mediator in disputes, it must first earn the trust of the people of the region. Our government's handling of World War II issues has been a hindrance. We must not only apologize in words but take action that will demonstrate our sincerity. There are any number of issues we should settle, though postwar reparations issues have already been resolved in international agreements. The government must take carefully considered measures to respond to those who were victims of the war and those who were left out of the prosperity that Japan enjoyed thereafter. The government will be responsible for these sorts of responses, but Japanese citizens, too, should undertake similar efforts in the private sector.

Resolution of the problems of the past is not enough to build confidence between nations. We need to develop bold policies intended to build trustful relations over the long term. Increasing the number of Asian students in Japan and our support for them would be one example. We should also continue to offer the nations of this region well-planned economic cooperation designed to meet their needs. Japan's economic influence here is overwhelming.

The nature of our cooperation in the years to come should emphasize the following three areas. First, we must increase the scope of our economic cooperation. Second, we must base our national and sectoral allotments on fundamental polices, and clarify what those issues are. For example, I believe we should begin to emphasize aid to such areas as Mongolia and Central Asia, which are moving toward democratization and market economies. We should also pay more attention to Vietnam. Third, Japanese cooperation should have a "Japanese flavor" distinct from American or European cooperation and should be based on our own recent experiences as a developing nation. The education and development of Official Development Assistance professionals should reflect this.

The Dawn of Multilateral Diplomacy

The post–Cold War security environment in Asia is fragile. We need to develop a new security framework that can respond to the power vacuum that would be left by an American withdrawal. To build mutual trust we need a fixed place where the many nations of this complex region—including Japan and the United States—can discuss security issues. A good starting point would be a permanent Asia-Pacific Ministerial Conference.

In July 1991 Foreign Minister Tarō Nakayama proposed that the Expanded ASEAN Foreign Ministers Meeting be the site for political discussions. His idea was that the Expanded ASEAN, including Japan and America, should become the basis for a regular Asia-Pacific Summit that would eventually embrace China, the Korean peninsula, Russia, and Central and South American nations. The organization could be called the Asia-Pacific Ministerial Conference.

The conference should discuss a number of regional issues. The list might include the prevention of regional disputes, mediation between disputing nations, peace-keeping operations following the resolution of disputes, military facilities, democratic development, and human rights in member nations. The conference could also serve as mediator between the United Nations and various bilateral relationships. Japan can expect the most cooperation from America at such a conference, followed by ASEAN and Oceania.

Japan is in a position to take a leadership role in such an arrangement. Our experience of atomic warfare puts us in a unique position to take the initiative in nuclear disarmament and in the creation of registration systems for the export of arms. Japan is an example of a nation that has developed economically without a major military force. We can work well with the nations of ASEAN and Oceania. These countries understand Japan's potential responsibility and role in the region; they did not oppose the Japanese deployment of mine sweepers to the Middle East or of PKO personnel elsewhere.

Malaysian Prime Minister Mohamad Mahathir remarked that "our old fear of Japan [becoming militarist again] has been reduced a great deal." Philippine President Fidel Ramos said that "Japan's personnel contribution to Cambodia is important, and we support it," and Indonesian President Sueharto has maintained that "it is natural that Japan would make efforts for peace." Newly elected Prime Minister Goh Chok Tong of Singapore also stated that he "represents a new generation and is too young to recall the Second World War." Such statements by ASEAN leaders have considerably deflated Chinese and Korean criticism that Japan's personnel contributions are signs of a renewed militarism. As a result, both China and Korea have begun to exhibit an "understanding" of Japanese personnel contributions that include the SDF.

Japanese diplomacy has hitherto been based on the U.S.–Japan alliance. In the Asia-Pacific region, too, bilateral relationships have been dominant. We have virtually no experience in multilateral diplomacy; it is the area in which we are least equipped. It is by embarking on multilateral diplomacy, however, that we can best fulfill our responsibilities in the region and grow into a fully functioning member of the international community in name and in substance.

CHAPTER SIX

Constructive Uses of
Foreign Aid

An Aid Superpower

I argued in Book I that if Japan remains a dinosaur with only a
small brain, it will be unable to adapt to the dramatic changes of
our times. We cannot remain a "faceless" nation "without clear
policies or goals." Yet we have not undertaken a serious discussion,
at the political level, of the kind of country we want to be, or of
how we want to be seen in the world. This lack of clarity is the
biggest problem in our Official Development Assistance.

In 1991 Japanese ODA totaled more than $10 billion, making
Japan the world's biggest donor. Japan's 0.32 percent proportion of
aid to GNP was higher than that of both the United States and
Britain, though still lower than the 0.7 percent goal of the United
Nations and slightly less than the 0.35 percent average of the
twenty member-nations of the Development Assistance Committee (DAC), a subsidiary organization of the OECD. It is almost
three times larger than it was ten years ago, and is growing at a rate
far beyond the average of DAC member nations. Again, whereas in
the 1970s only six developing countries listed Japan as their biggest
aid donor, by 1989, that figure had risen to thirty. Fifteen of these
countries were in Asia, and in fourteen of them, Japan provided
over half their total aid.

Japan intends to increase its ODA and to play a responsible role
as an economic power. However, if we do so only defensively to

avoid the criticism that we have pursued trade surpluses at the expense of others, our ODA will be stripped of all its positive significance. ODA is a valuable tool in peace-building efforts. We must treat it as such. ODA can assist in building not only industrial but social and cultural infrastructures. We can help nations to enlarge their educational and medical systems and to preserve their cultural inheritance. The assistance that enhances stability and economic development in developing nations will contribute to international peace and thereby to Japan's peace and prosperity. Our contributions will build trust for Japan in developing nations and a deeper understanding of our character as a nation. Instead of being "faceless," Japan will be understood to be contributing to world peace.

Our efforts will not gain recognition, however, if we simply pour in more money without clarifying our principles and intents. We must, at the political level, design an overarching vision for ODA, and we must make sure it is clear to all. Japan's ODA is based on the aid philosophy that says "help developing nations help themselves"; we select our aid programs based on requests from recipient nations. It is therefore all the more important that we not open ourselves to the criticism that our aid serves the business interests of Japanese companies.

Our decision-making process in ODA has been criticized. Formally, the cabinet makes the decisions, which are followed by exchanges of notes with the recipient nations and then by several stages of surveys. In reality, however, the finance, foreign affairs, and international trade and industry ministries and the Economic Planning Agency have already selected their aid projects. This is one reason for the criticism that our decision-making process is not sufficiently transparent. There is no room in such a process for a larger ODA strategy. The process should not be criticized merely because bureaucrats take the lead in it, but it does require a thorough review.

We should meanwhile be aware that some of the criticism of our ODA is misdirected. The Japanese government's lack of public relations on ODA is at least partly responsible for the misconceptions. Reports on a small number of failures are heavily emphasized in the press and contribute to a mistaken impression of ODA as a whole.

We also suffer a chronic scarcity of experienced people in everything from policy planning on aid to its implementation and subsequent evaluation. We need to develop people with expertise in these areas.

The Foreign Ministry's *Report Evaluating Economic Cooperation* also refers to frank criticisms of Japanese ODA by third parties: "There is no *ex post facto* examination of specific aid cases," and "ODA efforts are vast and sweeping. They lack careful, detailed consideration." Numbers alone will not earn Japan the appreciation it deserves for its ODA—we need experts who can improve the quality, not just the quantity, of the programs.

Japanese aid programs need some adjustments. They need to take into account the changes that have come with the end of the Cold War and the emergence of environmental issues. The swelling number of countries receiving aid poses problems. Not only is the number of developing nations in general on the rise, the recent democratization of Eastern Europe and the dissolution of the Soviet Union have produced a rapid increase in the total number of nations eligible for aid. In 1991 and 1992 alone, roughly twenty nations in Eastern Europe, the Baltics, and the former Soviet republics have joined the roster of aid recipients, and the nations of Indochina will soon join them.

The concept of aid has also broadened. There are new aims and needs, including those of environmental preservation projects. The participating nations of the 1992 Earth Summit agreed on the principle that ODA should be applied to environmental projects. Moreover, as the need for aid increases, we should be wary of "aid fatigue." The ratio of aid to GNP in America, for example, has fallen significantly in recent years. In this context, Japan is regarded as the most promising donor.

ODA as Part of Diplomatic Strategy

Given the changed aid environment, I believe that we must make ODA a consistent part of our diplomatic strategy for enhancing world peace and stability. We should provide ODA based on the following principles:

ONE: We must delineate the beliefs and principles guiding our aid plans and strategies. In our effort to "help developing nations help themselves," we have thus far formulated policies by reviewing and selecting from among the requests received from various nations. This particular path was chosen because of Japan's own experience and its experience of providing aid to Asian nations. This method has been both effective and useful. However, as the world's largest aid donor, Japan has a responsibility to demonstrate clearly the principles and aims governing our economic aid. We must spell out the kind of post–Cold War international society we seek as well as the particular role we anticipate our aid will play.

The "Four Kaifu Principles" of democratization, human rights, peace, and sustained development were articulated by the Kaifu administration in April 1991 with the view that aid should be used to realize the common aims of humanity in the wake of the Cold War. A little over a year later these four principles were further clarified in the Japan's Official Development Assistance Charter: 1) establish economic development and environmental preservation as the twin pillars of ODA; 2) prevent the use of ODA for military purposes; 3) guard against the use of ODA for military spending, development of missiles and other weapons of mass destruction, and the export and import of armaments; and 4) weigh efforts to promote democratization, the introduction of market economies, and the guarantee of human rights and liberty.

We must go beyond establishing principles and do our utmost to realize the principles in specific ODA policies and projects. The issues raised in The Four Kaifu Principles are intimately related to the security and internal problems of recipient nations. We have to give careful consideration to the actual conditions in each country.

The Development Assistance Committee of the OECD has already proposed requiring transparent accounting of military spending as a condition of aid to developing nations. If such concrete measures as reviews or suspensions of aid are to have any effect, however, donor nations have to be prepared to stand together to enforce them. Earlier I indicated the need for stricter supervision of the arms business; we must also consider suspending aid to nations that are exporting arms that threaten stability or peace, or that are producing or importing unnecessarily large volumes of armaments. Japan should take the lead in this area.

TWO: The increasing need for aid requires that Japan set priorities among recipient nations and sectors. We should build cooperative relations between government and private non-ODA capital, suppliers, international organizations, former recipient nations such as the Asian NIEs, and non-governmental organizations. Information on Japan's aid must be made public and readily available. The creation of a third-party organization that objectively evaluates the impact of our ODA would also be valuable.

Aid resources are limited. Japan should concentrate its aid in the sectors where contributions are particularly valuable. It should also be noted that Japanese ODA, concentrated mainly in industrial infrastructure such as electricity, transport, and telecommunications, has contributed a great deal to the economic development of many Asian nations. Aid in medicine and food will continue to be important in the future, but it is also essential that we assist recipient nations in becoming self-reliant. This is the most effective form of aid in the long term.

THREE: We must provide aid with regional security as our aim. For example, Japan can contribute to multilateral efforts to develop the Mekong River so that the five countries along the river—China, Laos, Thailand, Cambodia, and Vietnam—can use the river effectively. Efforts like this, which involve more than one country and an unstable political environment, require special commitment and determination. But if they are successful, they enhance regional stability. Such efforts by Japan will demonstrate to the people of the region our true position on peace and stability.

The recent agreement to impose a worldwide ban on the production of chemical weapons may create some hardship for developing nations that produce these weapons, and they may try to continue production in secret. Such concerns could be alleviated if, for example, Japan assisted in converting these factories to fertilizer production.

100,000 Foreign Students per Year

Another major component of our international efforts should be the area of human development. Before the war, Japan made active efforts to welcome foreign students. In the postwar period, those in leadership positions in countries that followed Japan in their development have mostly studied in Europe and America. We need to take steps immediately to increase the number of students coming to Japan.

We have established job-training centers in and sent technical instructors to various developing countries. Such technical assistance has borne fruit in this area of human development. We must now extend this assistance to provide education and vocational training in Japan to students and workers from developing nations.

Japan has had a myriad of opportunities to learn from foreign countries by sending people abroad, beginning centuries ago with trips to Sui and T'ang China, and continuing today in the form of government-funded travel to Europe and America. As many as 120,000 young people a year are sent by their families and businesses to study abroad.

In contrast, there are only about 40,000 foreign students studying at Japanese high schools and universities, though that number is now rising. Far more students go elsewhere, to nations that more readily accept them. America currently has some 360,000 foreign students. France receives about 140,000, and Germany takes in 90,000. Just as our students received education and the opportunity for intellectual development abroad, young people from other nations must be given the same opportunities by Japan. We have to throw our doors wide open to enable foreign students to achieve an excellent education and to learn about our traditions and culture.

I would like to see Japan take a minimum of 100,000 students annually by the year 2000. A good starting point for this goal is the expansion of a nationally funded system for foreign students. America currently receives 86,000 foreign students on federal monies. France accommodates 10,000. Japan only takes in 5,000. We should greatly expand that number. Second, national and local governments should offer subsidies or tax incentives to the private voluntary groups, companies, and schools that offer scholarships to foreign students.

A third important task is to develop a preparatory program for foreign students to ensure the scholastic background and information necessary to study here. We will have to send Japanese-language teachers abroad and develop an elective system for those who want to study in Japan. Systems should be in place in foreign countries to assist students who may want to enter Japanese high schools or universities.

Additionally, we need a system for receiving foreign students. Of particular importance is the development of a support structure to help cover medical costs incurred by foreign students. We must build more dormitories, but I strongly oppose the recent trend of building dormitories for the exclusive use of foreign students. Foreign students should not be segregated from Japanese students but should be offered the opportunity to live and study together with them.

The homestay and host-family system should be strengthened. Foreign students should have the chance to enter a Japanese family and live as Japanese children do. We must quickly arrange public support for host families and homestay go-between groups. In addition, it will be important to assist the students in their daily life. We should seriously consider establishing a public subsidy system for remedial Japanese lessons and other measures.

A Technical Training System for Foreign Workers

In recent years the number of foreigners coming to work in Japan has steadily increased. Thousands of young men and women come from abroad, hoping to earn a good income in prosperous Japan, to polish their skills, and to help their families back home. As with students, we should welcome their efforts by opening our doors further.

At the same time, taking in an unlimited number of foreign workers is unrealistic—something no country is willing to do. All countries have limits, great or small, on the entry of foreigners, based on economic, labor, and social conditions. Japan is no exception. The number of illegal foreign workers has also steadily risen. Many enter on tourist visas and work on construction sites, in factories, or as hostesses. The number of illegal workers is estimated at around 300,000 today, almost one-third the number of the 1,070,000 foreigners legally residing in Japan.

Regulation of such large numbers of people is virtually impossible, and their illegal status means they have to live in hiding. It also keeps them from going to the hospital or from requesting compensation for work-related injuries. Because they are here illegally, they often find themselves in the hands of cruel people who pay exploitative wages and demand long working hours.

More often than not, illegal foreign workers leave Japan with bitter memories of their stay. The negative feelings they have toward Japan are then communicated in some form to those at home. It would be very unfortunate if experiences like these were to mar relations between Japan and their home countries in the future. It is desirable for both Japan and for other countries that foreigners come here to work for their living, develop their technical skills, and use them to build their countries when they return home. One possible solution to this complex issue could be to create a comprehensive technical training system for foreign laborers.

This system should not serve simply as stopgap measure for Japan's labor shortages, but rather should enable foreign workers to use what they have learned in Japan to contribute to the economic development of their home countries. We already have one such program and plan to establish a new system in fiscal year 1993. Under the new system, the first three months of a foreign worker's stay in Japan will be spent learning Japanese and other skills. Living expenses for the period will be paid by the companies planning to employ them. After the three-month period, the workers sign employment contracts and embark on two years of technical training.

However, there are obvious flaws in this system. Now that the economic "bubble" has burst, we are closer to experiencing a labor surplus than a labor shortage. It is questionable to what extent companies will be willing to cooperate in a foreign-worker training program. The program must therefore have solid support from the national government. The government should, for example, pay the living expenses for the student's language-study period. After the employment contract is signed, the government can assist the company through tax and capital incentives. Companies will accordingly want to bring in foreigners. Of course, the mechanics of the program will also have to assure that it does not put pressure on Japanese workers.

We could also require the companies to present training plans for the two years and to report on training conditions. These requirements would help ensure that workers are assigned to appropriate companies and that they complete the program. Above all, their work in Japan must not begin and end with simple unskilled labor. We must be sure that they receive at least some advanced training. In construction, for example, this might include such skills as filling concrete molds, building steel frames, or operating construction equipment. Our aim is to avoid using foreigners as a cheap source of labor and instead assist them in developing their home countries.

Currently, the ministries of justice, foreign affairs, and labor all address foreign-labor issues separately. The resulting procedural requirements are often contradictory. Visas are not necessarily in accord with periods of stay under certain programs, for example. Foreign-worker training is ODA in the broadest sense of the term. It is an important part of foreign relations, and the ministries should unite in their handling of foreign labor.

Leadership in Environmental Preservation

It is common knowledge that the earth's natural environment is rapidly being destroyed. One of the major issues facing humanity at the end of the twentieth century is the protection of the earth from destruction and the recovery of a healthy and rich natural environment.

The 1972 declaration issued by the U.N. human environment conference in Stockholm put it this way:

> Of all things in the world, people are the most precious. It is the people ... that through their hard work, continuously transform the human environment. Along with social progress and the advance of production, science

and technology, the capability of man to improve the environment increases with each passing day.

However, environmental conditions have steadily worsened since this declaration. People somehow believe that they control the natural environment, that they have the right and the ability to use nature as they will. But the ubiquity of environmental destruction tells us that this conception of man's dominance of nature is profoundly mistaken. The day of reckoning is at hand, and we have no choice but to change our way of life.

The Western values that have driven the world are based on the idea that man dominates nature. The means by which man sought to control nature was scientific and technological development. It has resulted in today's mass-production, mass-consumption society. But we will shortly have no choice but to pay our accumulated debt to nature.

Clearly, we cannot regress to the pre-development age. Our aspiration should be to live a healthy and civilized life in a clean environment. A balance between environmental protection and economic development must be the resolution to this issue.

Japan is fortunate to have had the experience of battling and conquering pollution in the period of our rapid economic growth. We have had notable success in balancing environmental protection with economic growth through the united efforts of our government and our citizens to protect the environment and conserve energy. Japan is therefore particularly suited to leading the way in global environmental recovery. We must take the initiative in this area.

Our efforts cannot be confined to giving aid to developing nations for environmental protection. Whatever national borders exist in politics or economics, they are not shared by nature. We must protect the environment of the entire world if we are to live comfortably ourselves. This issue—along with personnel contributions in the security arena and economic aid—is one of the most important political issues facing Japan today.

The first thing Japan needs to do is survey the kinds of technical know-how it has and determine which skills are applicable to various types of problems. We need, in other words, an inventory of intellectual expertise that is applicable to environmental problems. The implementation stage will call for the participation and cooperation of experts and a wide variety of other people.

Today a number of Japanese organizations support environmental activity. MITI (Ministry of International Trade and Industry) and the Environment Agency have been promoting atmospheric and water pollution cleanup efforts as part of bilateral technical cooperation programs. The Japan International Cooperation Agency has been sending survey teams and private environmental experts to various places in Asia. Such programs are quite large in scale, even in comparison with those of other advanced nations. Organizations such as these should take the lead as we begin to implement new programs.

The call for widespread public participation is not intended simply to borrow the time and labor of people but to deepen public consciousness of environmental issues. Environmental protection begins with ordinary people cleaning up their immediate surroundings. If we care about the environment, we will conserve goods and energy and will resist the temptation to carelessly dispose of goods; we will actively engage in recycling. With heightened awareness, people will stop tossing cans by the roadside and cigarette butts into the street. These simple actions alone will improve our immediate environment and reduce waste.

Intellectual contributions to the environmental discussion are necessary as well. Japan's experience of environmental destruction during the period of rapid growth and of environmental recovery thereafter will be instructive regarding the environmental-destruction issues that have now assumed global proportions. It would thus be extremely useful to organize systematically the information available in each sector of the economy so that it can be made available to those who require it.

In addition to organizing a comprehensive research facility that could undertake that task, we must form a network among existing research organizations, including universities. Such a think tank would help people here and abroad make effective use of Japan's experience in their own environmental-protection and recovery efforts.

Environmental destruction is especially concentrated in the industrializing Asian nations. The entire region faces the same kind of pollution problem Japan had in the recent past, and could learn from Japan's experience. Solutions to environmental concerns in the Asia-Pacific region are very much in Japan's interest. An "Asian Environmental Cooperation Center" could form a valuable part of Japan's intellectual and technical aid and become the core of efforts to join Asian nations in environmental management.

The people, money, and knowledge available for environmental issues are limited. The effective use of these resources demands that environmental administration not be entirely scattered among the various countries; cooperation among nations will mean a higher level of environmental protection. Capital contributions to global issues like overseas aid and environmental protection will require careful planning. As with aid, the government should in principle make available sufficient financial resources for priority expenditures. There has been discussion of an environmental tax that could serve as a financial resource for international contributions; environmental taxes such as the petroleum tax designed to reduce consumption, however, should remain separate. I will discuss tax issues in detail in Book III, but let me simply say here that funds for foreign aid and environmental policies should first be based on a careful review of priorities and resource management and then supplemented from general funds based on income or consumption taxes.

THE FIVE FREEDOMS

The Japanese Dream

"We Wouldn't Want to Be Like the Japanese"

I once heard a well-known American intellectual say, "We wouldn't want to be like the Japanese." At first it sounded to me like an affront. But the more I thought about it, the less surprising the comment became. He was implicitly criticizing the huge gap between what appears to be our high income and what is in reality a poor standard of living. He was thinking of our inferior housing, impoverished social capital, high prices, long working hours, severe exam competition, and many other things. The European journalist who said "the Japanese live in rabbit hutches and spend all their time working" probably had the same things in mind.

Japan's rapid economic growth has often been referred to as a miracle. In less than fifty years, Japan raised itself from the ashes of war to become an economic superpower boasting one of the world's highest incomes. Nonetheless, the people living in this supposed economic giant do not feel as though they are leading rich lives.

In the Tokyo area, the dream of home ownership grows increasingly improbable, even with a lifetime of hard work toward that goal. There is something wrong with a society where people cannot buy proper homes no matter how hard they try. One of the primary aims of working people is to build a fine home of their own. Yet many young people have simply abandoned any hope of buying a home. This is a terrible state of affairs.

It is our political leadership that must take responsibility. Are we really a people whose standard of living ranks among the world's highest? Do citizens see this standard reflected in their own lives? Japanese enjoy a higher per capita income than either Americans or Europeans but, according to some surveys, when income is calculated relative to working hours or to prices, Japanese income is only about 70 percent that of America or Germany. Japanese may have a high income, but they work long hours for it and then see it eaten away in no time by the high price of goods.

Europeans and Americans have other things in mind as well when they say they don't want to be like the Japanese. One of our prime ministers was once ridiculed in Europe as just a "transistor salesman." Other familiar terms reflect the same impression: "economic animal" has become all but synonymous with Japan. Japan is regarded as a country whose only concern is economics, and as a nation whose competitiveness is extreme and destructive when carried out internationally. In the past, Japan was accused of "social dumping" or destroying Europe's domestic industries by launching export drives of cheap goods produced in Japan's exploitative labor market. Sixty years later, our image has barely changed.

Japan is already the world's largest donor of economic aid. But it is accused of relying solely on "checkbook diplomacy." Foreign laborers come to Japan to earn enough money to afford them a more affluent life in their own countries. They sometimes stay in Japan for years, but to them Japan is simply a place to earn money. They do not want to settle down here permanently.

Such images are of course often exaggerated and unrealistic. But they are not altogether false. The way foreigners evaluate us is an important barometer of the maturity of Japanese society. We will not be able to exercise leadership in international society as long as foreigners are unable to say that Japan is a laudable country, that they would like to live here or to build their countries on a Japanese model. We must therefore create our own "Japanese dream."

When America entered its golden age at the turn of the century,

American society with its "American dream" was the object of envy and longing to many people living overseas. America was a society driven by tremendous economic power, and the "dream" meant that anyone with ability and the willingness to work hard could have a chance to do well. America actively embraced immigrants and foreign students and spread its social, cultural, and economic influence throughout the world. Those who experienced American life wanted to bring its wonders home to their own countries. Our ancestors were among the many who thought they would like to make their countries like America.

In the realm of economic statistics, Japan is today running even with or even surpassing America. But one never hears anyone speak of a "Japanese dream."

Japanese Society Is Showing Signs of Strain

For all its faults, contemporary Japanese society does have much to be proud of. Its safety and stability are unmatched anywhere. People everywhere in the world yearn to live in a peaceful society largely free of violent crime. Japan has been able to provide such an environment for its citizens.

Japan should also be proud of its income distribution. The gap between rich and poor is exceptionally small. While recent speculation in land values has caused the gap to widen somewhat between those who own land and those who do not, Japan is one of the world's few societies to realize near equality in earned salaries, which undoubtedly contributes significantly to our social stability. Anyone who works in the conventional way can live without undue anxiety about his own life or his society. While this seems altogether obvious to Japanese, it is very important and worthy of note: few countries enjoy this degree of stability.

Japan is, in both good and bad ways, an extremely comfortable society. Japanese consumers are treated like royalty, and citizens are especially protected from the risks and shocks inherent in social life. In this sense, government regulations and intervention, though overly protective on the whole, have contributed significantly to social stability. We only realize the true value of a stable society when we look at the tragedy of nations that have lost social stability entirely.

The counterpart to these blessings is the poverty of the lives of citizens. Our economy and society are beginning to show signs of strain. The economy continues to grow, while the people—the very essence of the economy—are robbed of their freedom. Why is this? It is because Japan, in its pursuit of stability and efficiency, has become a society dedicated solely to its corporations. The people have become mere cogs in the Japanese corporate wheel.

Japanese people work long hours and are almost completely subject to the will of their companies. Companies retain most of the fruits of economic growth; the portion left to individuals is small by comparison. We may have nominally attained the world's highest income, but we continue to struggle with small residences, lengthy commutes, and extreme urban concentration. Various administrative programs and regulations are in place, ostensibly for the protection of the citizens, but to what extent do they truly serve the citizen? Even if they in fact once did, their utility today is in serious doubt.

Seen from overseas, permanent employment and the seniority system look like tools that have been used to bind people to their companies. An economic and social framework that emphasizes cooperative, long-term relationships seems nothing more than a closed society, one that bars foreign companies or any other outsiders from entering. This system—once regarded as an outstanding model—is increasingly showing signs of strain.

Becoming a Society that Values the Individual

The constraints on individual lives have become needlessly binding. The elimination of excessive restraints will allow the liberation of the individual, which is the most important task facing Japan's political leadership today.

I would like to see Japan strive toward the goal of "five freedoms."

• *Freedom from Tokyo* requires reversing the extreme concentration of population and resources in Tokyo and making the transition from urban overcrowding and rural depopulation to a more balanced development policy.

• *Freedom from companies* means placing the individual rather than the company at the center of the social and economic framework, so that each citizen can approach his or her work more freely and place greater value on his or her own individual life.

• *Freedom from overwork* requires steps that will aggressively reduce work hours so that people may work with greater ease and plan their own futures. We must also alter the excessively competitive examination system.

• *Freedom from ageism and sexism* means enabling the growing number of senior citizens to participate more fully in society, and building a society in which women can play more active and varied roles.

• *Freedom from regulation* entails abolishing anachronistic and meaningless rules. It also means allowing individuals and companies more freedom.

If we can achieve these five freedoms, we will release our citizens from their social and political shackles and begin to build a society that truly values the individual. Japan must become a society in which individuals can act freely, based on their own judgment. Respect for the individual does not refer only to oneself, but to a society that enables mutual self-respect and coexistence among individuals. Individual freedom will mean a society that offers many choices, a society that not only permits but encourages diversity.

Unnecessary regulations must be recognized as such and eliminated as quickly as possible. Companies and individuals must act more autonomously. The power that has been concentrated in the capital must be decentralized; local areas must make their own decisions and turn Japan into a society that embraces diversity. We must put all our effort into rectifying our extreme Tokyo-centrism, whose distorted form of efficiency has hampered improvements in ordinary life. Senior citizens and women, who are today bound by too many social restrictions to participate to their full potential in society, must be accorded greater freedom. We must also contain the excesses of corporate behavior that today so distort individual lives.

The release of people from what is effectively a protective but confining social incubator is long overdue. This will, of course, require that people take responsibility for themselves, but this should not be considered undesirable. There should be no freedom of choice without a sense of responsibility for self. We must make available whatever information will allow individuals to make their own choices and take responsibility for their own lives. That is the meaning of a free society.

What kind of society will Japan be if we liberate people from their tethers and proclaim these five freedoms? It will depend on the choices each individual citizen makes. When diversity flourishes, the content of a gratifying and prosperous life will differ according to the individual.

Government should have little to say about individual choice. What is required of government is not that it offer citizens a ready-made "affluent life." It should instead eliminate the barriers to individual action and provide an environment in which people can use their own power as they see fit to construct the kind of lives they want. This is the intent of the five freedoms I am calling for. If we can attain these freedoms, the appropriate course toward rich and meaningful lives will open before us of its own accord. The question is how to do it.

CHAPTER TWO

Freedom from Tokyo

30,000 Hours of "Commuter Hell"

The average one-way commuting time for office workers in Tokyo is now approximately ninety minutes. Assuming that an average office worker has two days off per week, works fifty weeks a year, and stays at his job for forty years, he will have spent 30,000 hours (1,250 twenty-four-hour days, or three and a half years) commuting. This huge loss of time essentially means that Tokyo residents have become "commuter slaves." The overcrowding problem brought about by the extreme population concentration in the Tokyo area has reached its limits.

While the congestion grows worse in the big cities, the countryside suffers severe depopulation. "Depopulation" does not refer only to the decrease in the rural population. It also means that the generational balance in the countryside is collapsing. As more and more young people move to the cities, the rural population ages rapidly. The eventual outcome of this pattern will be the destruction of regional society and the loss of its financial, industrial, and cultural foundations. It will mean the end of many potentially thriving industries. We already see such consequences in the forestry industry, which, although prosperous today, is threatened by the steady outflow of workers.

Until recently, the various regions of Japan had their own unique features and autonomous communities. This social and cultural diversity was Japan's heritage. Depopulation destroys that heritage and suffocates the very roots of these regions. It is no exaggeration to say that the postwar Japanese economy was built on the strength of these areas. Throngs of people—many of whom would eventually lead Japan—left the countryside for Tokyo. They were the source of Japan's high productivity and quality products. Now, all the strength of these regions—all the nutrients—has been drained by Tokyo. Our non-urban regions are dying.

We should take the issues of urban concentration and rural depopulation very seriously. Japan is a small nation: 120 million of us live cheek-by-jowl in what is already a small area. Why must we all congregate in the still narrower confines of the capital? A healthy future for Japanese society demands that we create a sensitive balance between urban and rural. This balance has already broken down, and we need to recover it.

Tokyo has become something of a monster. The people of Japan have to be liberated from its grip. To this end, we must undertake tax reform, invest in social overhead capital, and commence the decentralization that I discussed in Book I. Without freedom from Tokyo, Japan will not be able to build an affluent society for the twenty-first century.

The Limits of Unipolar Concentration

The extreme concentration in the big cities—particularly in Tokyo—is not simply a matter of overcrowding. "Unipolar concentration" refers to the fact that virtually all functions of society, including economic, political, and cultural, are intertwined and concentrated in a single place. The difficulty of disentangling these functions from each other prevents us from correcting the excesses of Tokyo-centrism.

Scores of companies, for example, have brought their headquarters to Tokyo or expanded their Tokyo operations. As our industrial base shifts to the tertiary sector, industries such as finance and communications—necessarily based in Tokyo—assume increasing importance, exacerbating Tokyo's omnipresence. Most of the nation's products also flow into Tokyo, the main consumption center of Japan.

Government is perhaps even more concentrated in Tokyo. Following the war, the administration of Japan was located in Kasumigaseki, in central Tokyo. The administrative system was divided vertically: Kasumigaseki was the base from which all administrative organizations stretched their tentacles out to control every last nook and cranny of the country. This is true of education, transportation, construction, agriculture, finance, trade, and almost everything else of administrative concern. Tokyo-centric concentration is pressing forward in the cultural realm as well. The worlds of music, literature, and other arts are all concentrated in Tokyo.

Political, economic, and cultural concentration in Tokyo reinforce each other. Their interaction accelerates the convergence. Companies shift their headquarters to Tokyo, for example, to be near the administrative institutions located there. As economic activities in the capital expand—bringing more people to Tokyo in the process—cultural activities there also proliferate. The universities concentrated in Tokyo draw young people from other areas; graduates choose to stay and seek work in the capital. Even if they wanted to, they would not find work in their hometowns; the concentration of economic activity in Tokyo is simply too pervasive. The unipolar concentration of business and culture adds to Kasumigaseki's efficiency, and thereby to political concentration.

This unipolar concentration actually helped sustain the economic growth of postwar Japan. The administrative system launched Japan on a course of rapid economic development that required tremendous social capital, and centralized administration was therefore an extremely efficient formula for achieving this goal. The convergence of corporate activities in Tokyo was convenient for the exchange of information and personnel among companies, and promoted widespread industrial dynamism. Tokyo's universities, meanwhile, provided a steady stream of talented people to support such corporate activities.

Housing for the Cities, Employment for the Provinces

It is easy to criticize unipolar concentration. But it is difficult to correct, precisely because it is so economically efficient. The draw of Tokyo for anyone seeking information of any kind, for example, is beyond measure. The "information age" is already upon us; urban concentration, especially in the capital, will only increase unless we act now.

Japan could take one of two routes. First, we could assume that unipolar concentration is a natural process and stop fighting it. We could henceforth focus all social investment in, say, a three-hundred-kilometer area around the capital, a proposition strongly advocated by some economists. With extensive enough investment in roads, residences, public works, sewage, etc., the Tokyo metropolitan area could probably become a pleasant enough environment. Public investment could be carried out more efficiently, given its concentration in a single area. There is a great deal of waste in the way land is used in and near Tokyo. If we modified our land-use policies and made the necessary investments in social overhead capital, the living environment would improve significantly. We must recognize, however, that this would not solve the problem of depopulation and disintegration of other parts of the country.

The second choice is to suppress further concentration of population in Tokyo and to focus our efforts on balanced decentralization. Specifically, we must create multiple centers of industrial activity so as to expand employment opportunities outside Tokyo. With a reduction of industrial activities in Tokyo, those workers who remained in the capital would be better able to afford homes. Our aim would be to shift economic power to other areas, something that would not be possible without a fundamental and thoroughgoing shift in policy. The government has already made some attempts to halt the flow into Tokyo and to promote decentralization, but the unipolar concentration shows no signs of abating. Businesses rely too heavily on the efficiency that concentration offers.

Which road should we take? The answer, I think, is obvious. No matter how difficult decentralization will be, it is our only choice.

The other option, that of an ever-larger capital region, is simply an extension of the Japanese economic structure that generated rapid growth. It would mean that politics, economics, and culture would converge ever more insistently, producing an even more uniform society. An urban nation of this kind may boast high efficiency in production, but this is no longer the priority it once was. It has been superseded by the search for a higher quality of life.

Further urban concentration presents a host of other problems. We can hardly expect, for example, to be able to respond to such problems of high-density living as housing, commuting, garbage, and sewage when unipolar concentration becomes even more intensified. Certainly we must question the wisdom of crowding all our economic and other activities into a single place, given Japan's vulnerability to major earthquakes.

The future of Tokyo-centered concentration once again calls to mind the history of the dinosaurs. The dinosaur began as a simple creature, but gradually developed its functions and grew larger and larger. When its environment could no longer support it, however, it was doomed. The same is true of companies and organizations that become outsized through a kind of self-expansion mechanism: they too self-destruct. The same process applies equally to urban growth. A healthy system should have a balance between concentration and dispersion. Animals, organizations, and cities all have to try to maintain this balance. But they also undergo diffusion. There is no question that unipolar concentration in Tokyo has gone too far.

We need to develop long-term land policies that will achieve a more balanced development throughout the country. Policies can no longer be confined simply to questions of how to allocate social capital investment. They must cover a wide range of issues including changes in the industrial landscape, a review of Japan's cultural and educational foundations, and the alteration of the nature of administrative organizations.

In the short term, it will be extremely expensive to disperse the many functions of society to other areas. Regionally disparate economic development, however, promises innumerable advantages, as is evident in the healthy regional communities that exist today. Where there are special regional and cultural qualities, they can be passed on to future generations. Where land is used more effectively, people enjoy a closer relationship with nature and a better residential environment. Japanese society can pursue this diversity in regional development and reap the benefits of the choices that will result. A pluralistic and richly varied society is infinitely preferable to drawing all of society into one giant economic machine.

Decentralized living also allows people to develop deeper human relationships with each other. Currently, grandparents living in the country cannot see their urban grandchildren more than once a year. No matter how much energy we put into developing inexpensive rail and air routes, people cannot maintain close ties across very great distances.

The government has already made a number of attempts to contain the excessive concentration in Tokyo. It has emphasized investment in other regions. It has carried out projects like the "New Industrial Cities" in every region as incentives for regionally based companies and industries to stay where they are. In spite of these efforts, the government has been unable to halt the unipolar concentration in Tokyo. What should we do about this?

As I explained earlier, I believe we need a fundamental conceptual transformation regarding our administrative framework and, especially, regional self-rule. We will not stop unipolar concentration simply by building up social overhead capital outside Tokyo. We need a transformation in our very ideas. We must not only shift our investment allocations, we must reform Kasumigaseki's vertically divided administrative system so that the various regions can rely on their own wisdom to carry out regional administration. This is the only way we can hope to see diversification and the social decentralization of Japan. If we fail to make this shift, we will be unable to liberate ourselves from the meshes of Tokyo's unipolar concentration.

Generous Investment in Our Residential Environment

National policy will be of critical importance in the few years remaining of this century. We will have to carry out bold programs of public works investment—especially to lay the foundations of residential life—to serve what will be the most aged society in the world by the early twenty-first century. Programs such as these will form part of our planning for regional decentralization and for the stabilization of our industry and population. This is necessary in order to apply the brakes to Tokyo's urban concentration and also to ensure that we provide the necessary social capital for residential life throughout the country. If we fail to do so, we will see the serious destabilization of our population just when we are confronted with challenges posed by a rapidly aging society. If we delay reforms any longer, Japan's standard of living will continue to suffer in comparison with those of other advanced nations, and we will be risking a decline in the very strength of our nation.

The roots of today's recession are structural. The economy will not recover through tinkering. A bold public investment program is what is needed to prevent a further downturn in the business cycle. If we stimulate demand through our public investment, we will alleviate the rise in our trade surplus and thus ease the trade friction we experience with other nations. The primary components of public investment should include the following.

• *Expanded shinkansen networks.* The main project in public investment should be the construction of a national network of bullet trains (*shinkansen*), running from Hokkaidō to Kyūshū and along the Japan Sea, based on those plans already under consideration. Once built, they will make virtually any point in the Japanese archipelago quickly accessible. The shinkansen stops will become the core cities that bring development to their regions.

• *Better airports.* We should expand the airport facilities of the major cities throughout the country. The airline network has focused far too much on Narita (Tokyo), which has by now reached its limits. Odd as it may sound, it is more convenient for people in the country to go to America and Europe via Seoul than through Tokyo's airports. In addition to the Kansai airport currently under construction, we need to have international airports in Tōhoku, Hokuriku, Hokkaidō, Kantō, Chūbu, Chūgoku, Shikoku, and Kyūshū.

• *More expressways.* We must construct a network of expressways that will link all parts of the nation by early in the next century. This network will help improve contact between different regions and bind various parts of the country together. Today's expressway network converges on Tokyo, but we urgently need roads connecting other cities with each other.

• *Optical fiber grids.* We must prepare the facilities necessary for the optical fiber networks that will be a key part of the infrastructure of the twenty-first century. A single fiber just one-tenth of a millimeter in diameter can carry virtually unlimited amounts of information. Optical fiber will change human life in countless ways with high-density telephone and facsimile services, rapid computer transmissions, and high-density televisions with hundreds of channels. For maximum utilization of such networks we must immediately begin to develop the technical and intellectual skills to make the switch to these networks and create the software to run them. The aggressive development of our national information networks is essential to solidifying our standing as a world economic leader and to eliminating the great information gaps between the country and cities.

• *Improved facilities in non-metropolitan areas.* We have to lay a solid foundation for residential life in small cities and the countryside. The main reason that young urban men and women use to explain their dislike of the country is the lack of flush toilets. If we want to bring our young people back to their native regions, we must begin by building proper sewage facilities. By the year 2000 at

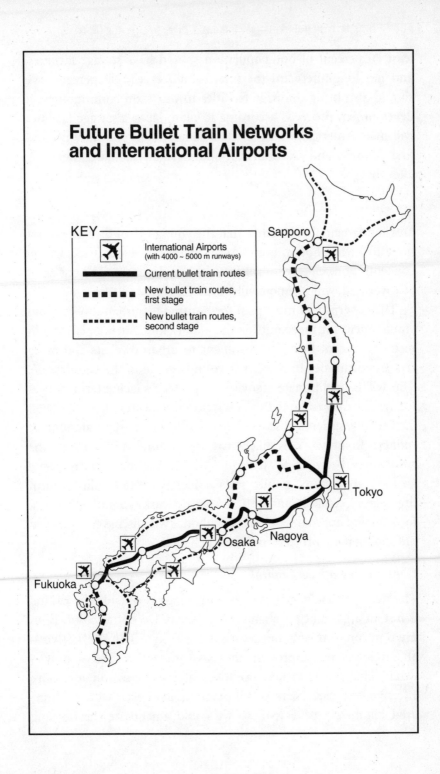

Future Bullet Train Networks and International Airports

KEY

✈ International Airports
(with 4000 ~ 5000 m runways)

━━━ Current bullet train routes

▬ ▬ ▬ New bullet train routes, first stage

- - - New bullet train routes, second stage

Sapporo

Tokyo

Nagoya

Osaka

Fukuoka

least 70 percent of our population should have sewage facilities, and not long afterward the total should exceed 90 percent. We should also bring drainage facilities to our farm communities. If development proceeds according to plan, Japan's sewage facilities will meet American and Canadian standards by the early twenty-first century, and reach British and German standards not long after that.

Our fundamental problem is that the young urban dweller cannot hope to own a house, even after a lifetime of hard work. Urban concentration, chiefly in Tokyo, is the main cause. The big cities are overused, while remote villages suffer disuse.

The government must plan for housing for urban dwellers and employment for those outside the major cities. Such a plan would restore a decent living environment to urban dwellers and bring rich opportunities to ambitious young people in the countryside. This will help eliminate many of the problems facing farm villages today. The only route to this end is public investment.

The investments discussed here will cost a huge amount of money. Road work is likely to cost around ¥52 trillion, the *shinkansen* between ¥7 trillion and ¥12 trillion, international airports ¥6 trillion, public sewage facilities ¥100 trillion, farm drainage ¥23 trillion, and optical fiber networks about ¥30 trillion, for a total of approximately ¥200 trillion. I will discuss the question of funding these projects in the next chapter.

Constructing a New Capital

The need for social diversification into areas outside the capital is not an argument for abandoning Tokyo. Decentralization is, in my opinion, our only hope for saving Tokyo. The alternative— an emphasis on improving the environment of Tokyo only— would likely include tax incentives and deregulation for more effective land use. There is still plenty of land even within a hundred kilometers of Tokyo, so we could ameliorate the housing problem if we laid more commuter lines to Tokyo.

Such prescriptions for Tokyo's ills are meaningless. The bigger Tokyo grows, the faster concentration will progress, until the vicious circle brings us back to where we started. Tokyo's density can only be moderated by developing appealing provincial cities, containing Tokyo's growth, and promoting the outflow of population to other areas. Tokyo will always remain the nation's financial and information center, but we have to get over the notion that it's necessary to bring anything and everything into the capital.

The creation of interesting and diverse cities is desirable for Tokyo residents as well as for non-Tokyo residents. Many people today cannot leave Tokyo even if they want to. They are dissatisfied with Tokyo life because of everything from inadequate housing to long commutes, but they cannot realistically hope to find employment opportunities at salary levels comparable to those for Tokyo's mid-career workers. This problem is especially acute for those raising children in Tokyo. When workers are transferred out of Tokyo by their companies, they frequently have no choice but to leave their wives and children behind in Tokyo because education elsewhere is considered inferior. The result is divided families, an extremely Japanese (and unnatural) way of life.

Conversely, a multipolar society, dispersed throughout the country, will widen the range of possibilities available to individuals and weaken the grip Tokyo has on Japanese citizens. People may choose small university towns for their college years and then work in the big city after graduation. When they marry and begin to raise children, they may favor areas with plenty of space and a rich natural environment. As they age, they may wish to retire where the climate is milder. In America, life planning of this sort is regarded as a given. It is simply how people live. But it is not possible in Japan today. Naturally, there will always be plenty of people who prefer to live their entire lives only in Tokyo or only in some other place. The point is that people should have the opportunity to choose.

This discussion of balanced development necessarily leads us to the question of moving the capital. I am certainly in favor of such a move. There are not many reasons to leave administrative and political functions in Tokyo. Political and economic centers are separate in many countries, including Germany, America, Canada, and Australia. Tokyo's extreme overpopulation suggests that the capital should be moved.

Such a move will constitute for Japan one of the great undertakings of the twenty-first century. It should therefore be on an appropriate scale. If we build a new capital, let it be something worthy of being passed on to posterity. Our own historic capitals at Heijō-kyō, Heian-kyō, Kamakura, and Edo remained as legacies to later generations; a twenty-first century capital, too, should live on. We may be the generation fortunate enough to carry out this task. It would be magnificent work to be a part of.

We must not, however, delude ourselves into thinking that moving the capital will be enough to resolve the problem of unipolar concentration in Tokyo. Our aim should not be the creation of a second Tokyo but rather a fundamental systemic reform in which administration is moved out of Tokyo and development is spread throughout the country. The move must be just one part of a larger, more thorough reform.

Freedom from Companies

Company Freedom, Individual Confinement

As corporations in Japan become more and more prosperous, their individual employees become less and less free. This is commonly believed to be true. Most people think that all good things—good land, good food, good recreation facilities—are swept up by corporations. That is why it is impossible for individuals to buy proper homes in the capital region, and why young people abandon the idea of buying their own homes and opt instead to enter companies that offer company housing. The proper order of things is reversed if workers are owned like pets by their companies and housing is offered as the equivalent of dog food.

Japan today must transfer corporate wealth to individuals. The first issue to address is the housing situation. Land prices in the best parts of the city are extremely inflated because of company demand for office space. When prices skyrocketed, people who once lived in such areas had no choice but to leave. They accordingly moved to the suburbs, and soon land prices in the Tokyo suburb of Setagaya and other areas began to climb. Moreover, companies also buy up suburban land for worker residences and recreational facilities. Housing available to ordinary individuals thus moves farther and farther away from the center of town. Land prices are unbelievably high even in suburbs ninety minutes from Tokyo by train. Those fortunate enough to purchase a house look forward to a lifelong struggle with loans and a total of thirty thousand hours of commuting time.

Company money also controls the free time that should, in theory, make our lives more comfortable. Exclusive clubs and the best restaurants costing ¥30,000–¥50,000 per person are available only to those on corporate expense accounts. Golf might be a pleasant recreation for older people, but only corporations can afford the membership fees charged at golf clubs near the capital. One after another, first-rate resorts also seem to end up as company facilities. Similarly, a majority of the luxury cars sold during the bubble period were bought on company funds as displays of corporate wealth and power.

While companies grow stronger and stronger, many of the people working in them find their lives entirely dictated by the demands of the company. It is unacceptable that people are unable to acquire decent housing in the Tokyo area unless they work at companies that offer company housing. People who eat unimaginably costly dinners on expense accounts cannot hope to enjoy such meals with those who are truly important, namely their families.

It is natural in a free-market economy that money confers power. But the argument that individuals who want the privileges that come with corporate money should join the strong, rich companies is naively simple. Individuals involved with corporations are eventually absorbed by them. Their own values do not receive adequate respect; individual needs are often sacrificed. Workers receive notices of transfers to distant places in a single memo; families are divided because of the transfers; promises of shorter working hours never materialize; overtime is demanded free of charge; people even die from overwork. All these problems have the same root cause.

Japanese corporations came through the period of rapid economic growth stronger than ever. The high earnings of strong companies should have gone toward improving the lives of the workers who bear the burden of corporate activities. Personal incomes have risen a great deal since the rapid growth period, but people do not feel as if they live in affluence.

Corporations are ostensibly the means by which people participate in economic society. Yet corporate organization has taken on a life of its own. Company imperatives have come to take priority over the values of working people. It may seem inevitable in capitalism that society should give priority to company values, but do people in Europe and America work overtime without compensation? Are their expense accounts as pervasive as Japan's? Are people there unable to have homes other than rented company housing? Is it a foregone conclusion that fathers will live far away from their children? The fact that individual lives are so bound to corporate needs is clearly due to serious flaws in the system.

Individuals have to be liberated from their companies. It is only when each individual becomes able to act autonomously that we will see the birth of a richly diverse and dynamic society.

Going Beyond the Rapid Growth Era

What I have just described is in no way a traditional Japanese construct. It is something that developed during the period of rapid growth.

The Japanese-style company system, with its cooperative industrial relations, long-term technical training, and stable employment, made Japan's rapid economic growth possible. Its permanent employment system, seniority wage structures, in-house technical training, and other features were also in some ways quite comfortable for the workers within this framework.

When Japan was trying to industrialize and "catch up" with the West, its first priority was to strengthen the corporate body. It was assumed that the lives of workers would naturally improve as companies prospered. This framework served economic development extremely well. Without this structure, the "miracle" of Japanese development would not have been possible.

Japan is no longer catching up. We now rank alongside the United States as an economic power. The social framework tied to rapid growth is no longer appropriate.

No one is entirely satisfied with the status quo. There are many calls for change from throughout society. One example is the movement by both companies and workers to shorten working hours. I will cover this subject in more detail later, but let me point out here that this is not simply a matter of establishing a shorter work day. It is an enormously complicated problem involving the very nature of Japanese society.

The increasing fluidity of the labor market is another sign that postwar ways are changing. Many people no longer orient their lives entirely around their companies; they focus instead on themselves and their families. They are beginning to recognize that their companies should be revolving around them. Many are changing jobs, a step virtually unheard of just a few years ago. Others are eagerly improving their skills or are participating in activities outside work such as social services. These are signs of forthcoming change.

External factors have changed as well. The social advancement of women is making progress; the male labor force is aging. More and more foreigners come to work in Japan. These kinds of developments are accelerating the transformation of the rapid growth–era company system. The internationalization of the Japanese economy is itself becoming an engine of change in Japanese employment. One of the issues of the Japanese company system is the difficulty experienced by new entrants, such as foreign companies, into the market. One reason is that companies setting up operations in Japan have trouble finding capable, experienced workers. If Japan's economy is really internationalizing, we may expect major transformations in our industrial society.

These kinds of changes will almost certainly affect the Japanese labor market. We should not sit passively by, letting events unfold as they will. We should actively take part in correcting the distortions of today's corporate society. Let there be no misunderstanding: the direction of change I am describing does not constitute a denial of corporate importance. Obviously, company activities will continue to be vitally important for the healthy development of the

Japanese economy. However, if we wish to maintain today's high productivity levels, we must rethink the relationship between company and individual. It is by giving individuals sufficient freedom and building healthy relationships between them and their companies that Japanese companies will be able to retain their dynamism over the long term.

The Severity of Individual Taxes

Japan's tax system is one of the major contributors to the social structure that subjugates individual to company needs. The ratio between direct and indirect taxes is too high here; direct taxes such as income taxes are a higher proportion of total taxes in Japan than in Europe. The tax system also clearly discriminates between individuals and corporations in favor of the latter. It does so by limiting the portion of company profits allotted either to workers or to stockholders, while permitting company holdings and expense account spending to climb.

One example of the discriminatory features of the tax system is in housing. An individual purchasing a home does so with after-tax income. Companies, in contrast, offer housing to employees as part of a benefits package and can thus regard interest on purchasing capital as an operating cost.

The bequests of real estate from individuals to their children are subject to inheritance taxes. So much so, in fact, that it is said any family assets will have been eaten up by the inheritance tax by the third generation. Company housing and buildings are not subject to similar taxes. Given this kind of discrimination, the best land will all eventually wind up as corporate assets.

Tax discrimination between individuals and corporations does not apply only to the acquisition of real estate. Automobile purchases are treated completely differently by the tax system depending on whether they are individual or company purchases. The same is true of stock investments. Corporations can write off large losses in the stock market, but individuals are not permitted to take these deductions.

The predominance of direct taxes also contributes to corporate power. With a system of high individual income tax rates, a sizable portion of what the company pays out in the form of wages is eaten up by taxes. It is thus cheaper for companies to pay their people in housing, company cars, and expense accounts than in actual wages. In short, the tax framework encourages companies to spend money on things other than increases in worker wages.

Today's steeply progressive individual income tax was devised in the postwar period when Japan was just rising out of poverty. It was designed to tax the wealthy heavily and to distribute that money widely—certainly a laudable aim. Now, however, as we seek new levels of affluence, the priorities and methods embedded in the tax system are no longer rational. Because income tax rates rise so steeply, people enjoy less than half of any additional income they earn. We should not assume that only the very few—the exceptionally rich—are in the higher tax brackets. A considerable number of people already fall into this range at today's income levels, and more and more young "salarymen" are likely to join their ranks as the seniority system disintegrates.

We urgently need a large-scale cut in income taxes. Our society is aging more rapidly than that of any other industrialized nation. The proportion of the population over age 65 was 9.1 percent in 1980, the lowest rate among industrialized nations, but by the year 2000 it will have passed those of the United States, Britain, and France at 16.9 percent. By 2020, it is expected to reach 25.2 percent. At present, the ratio of working people aged 20–64 to senior citizens is 5.5 to one. It is expected that, by the year 2020, only 2.1 working people will support each senior citizen. Medical, pension, and other social spending will increase as our society ages, but the proportion of working people who will be called on to pay for such costs will decrease rapidly. At today's tax rates, the income tax burden on working people will only grow heavier. Those currently working have to be uneasy about the prospects for Japan's welfare system in the early twenty-first century.

It should be noted here that, even today, the average elderly person enjoys greater material comfort than do most working people. Elderly households have lower annual incomes, but their income per household member is higher. The tax system offers senior's deductions, deductions for public pensions, and exemptions of ¥2 million more than those offered income-earning households. Furthermore, since housing loans and educational expenses for senior citizens are low, the proportion of income they spend on self-improvement and entertainment is high. Elderly people thus enjoy greater comfort and consume more. I raise these points to show that we cannot lay the tax burden entirely on the working generation but must achieve a better balance through the use of indirect taxes.

In sum, we must reform today's tax system, which too heavily favors corporations; we must greatly reduce income taxes and expand the range of choices available to individuals.

Cutting Income and Residence Taxes in Half

First, income and residence taxes should be cut in half. Because of the progressive income tax scale, the individual tax burden rises steadily with income even if individual income and residence tax rates remain at their current level. Working families, already struggling with mortgage payments and educational expenses, are particularly hit with this burden. We certainly cannot afford to undermine the will to work through *increased* tax burdens, given that our working population will begin to contract. High individual taxes can only aggravate the imbalance between salaried workers and others, threatening the very stability of our society. Cutting income and residence taxes in half will put a much larger chunk of disposable income into the hands of individuals, who would freely choose how to spend their own money.

Second, we must reduce the corporate tax to the lowest levels in the world. At the same time, we must strictly enforce corporate tax laws. Tax loopholes involving company recreational facilities, company residences, autos, expense accounts, and the various benefits added to the income of workers should not be permitted. The tax system should not allow owner-managers to use company facilities for private purposes.

Some people have suggested that corporate taxes be increased. But as the economy becomes more international, our tax system will have to take into account external as well as domestic conditions. If Japan stands out as especially costly in terms of corporate and asset taxes, companies and capital will flow to other nations. We cannot set corporate and asset taxes in isolation from the tax systems of other industrialized nations. We must, at the very least, be neutral in active international economic transactions. Lower rates would be better still.

The government obviously cannot cut income taxes in half without another means of generating income. Japan's tax system is peculiar among those of the twenty-four advanced industrialized nations of the OECD. Our income taxes make up a larger share of the total tax burden than in any other OECD country, and our consumption taxes the smallest share. We will not be able to avoid dealing with this issue in the coming years. We will somehow have to rectify this balance, and the most rational approach will be to increase the consumption tax rate.

While cutting income and residence taxes by half, we should raise the current 3 percent consumption tax rate to the 10 percent level (VAT or sales tax) established by our European and American counterparts. By raising consumption taxes and lowering income taxes, we will not only improve the balance between direct and indirect taxes but will also galvanize the will to work and expand individual choice in the use of disposable income. We will also thus be assured of funds for the investment in residential facilities that I discussed in Chapter 2. In other words, this tax reform is fully consistent with the aims of "freedom from companies" and "freedom from Tokyo."

If the economy continues in its current state, we might want to defer the consumption tax hike for two or three years after income taxes have been cut. We can make up the tax shortfall during this period by issuing deficit bonds. Specifically, tax revenue increases accruing to every 1 percent of consumption tax come to ¥1.8 trillion (calculations are based on the budget of fiscal year 1993). With special revenues of approximately half a trillion yen, the total increase comes to ¥2.3 trillion. Revenue increases should reach ¥3.2 trillion by fiscal year 2000. What will happen to average revenues between now and then?

Since consumption rates depend on the consumption tax rate, it is impossible to make accurate projections, but a very crude calculation suggests that if consumption taxes were raised from 7 percent to 10 percent, revenue increases could be expected to reach ¥20 trillion.

How much will we need to make up for the shortfall from other taxes? Calculations of only income and operating taxes based on the fiscal year 1993 budget show revenues of about ¥16 trillion. If we reduce income and operating taxes by half, we will need to raise ¥8 trillion. Individual residence taxes today total ¥8 trillion, so a 50-percent cut will mean a ¥4-trillion shortfall. Again, if corporate taxes are reduced from today's 37.5 percent to 33 percent, we lose ¥2 trillion, for a total shortfall of ¥14 trillion.

These are rough calculations that may not correspond exactly with the actual figures. Currently, the proportion of total tax revenue that comes from direct taxes tops 70 percent. The changes I have proposed should reduce the proportion to 60 percent. Even with the cuts in income, residence, and corporate taxes, these calculations suggest that a 10-percent consumption tax will generate ¥6 trillion in additional revenues. ¥5 trillion of this should be spent on public works investment for the next century.

The remaining ¥1 trillion may be used to defray the costs of fulfilling our global responsibilities. These include contributions other than ODA, such as projects furthering Japan–U.S. or Japan-European relations or the education and training of foreign students and laborers. We could also apply this money to other needs related to foreign relations, such as compensation to those hurt by market-opening measures and funds for small business and agriculture.

CHAPTER FOUR

Freedom from Overwork

Planning Our Own Futures

"Children study too hard, adults work too hard, and senior citizens have nothing to do," goes the common complaint. The "three excesses" accurately describe the problems facing Japanese society today. Children spend all their energy on the passive acquisition of data and math skills for the looming entrance-exam wars. After graduation, they devote themselves to their companies. Years later, retirement often brings little but boredom and an excess of free time.

This system has served Japanese industry well. The seemingly efficient use of people was a critical element in Japan's rapid development. Today, however, Japan is criticized by other countries as a nation that insists always on winning, as an "economic animal" that knows nothing outside the realm of hard work. This is why informed people from overseas say they "would not want to be like the Japanese."

More importantly, Japanese people themselves are beginning to express grave doubts about spending their entire lives as part of a production machine. Everyone wants an end to the "three excesses." Educational, labor, and social reform are all necessary solutions to these problems.

The Japanese labor market today faces a number of pressing problems. In the short term, we must reduce working hours; medium-term efforts should focus on laying the groundwork for the employment of senior citizens and women; and, over the long term, we must turn our company-centered society into one centered on the individual.

At first glance, these issues appear to be unrelated, but they are in reality intimately connected. If we do not reduce working hours, for example, we cannot promote the employment of senior citizens and women. If we want to create a working environment that welcomes senior citizens and women, we must reform Japan's corporate-centered society.

Contradictory as it may sound, the only way to maintain the dynamism of Japanese industry in a high-technology age is to liberate ourselves from overwork. We must enable people to spend more time on their own activities and choices instead of merely binding themselves to their work.

Three Reasons for Shorter Working Hours

There are at least three compelling reasons why we need to develop concrete policies aimed at reducing work hours. Above all, we need to bridge the gap between what is nominally the world's highest income level and our own sense that we do not lead affluent lives. In other words, while Japan enjoys almost an overabundance of material goods, the choices available to the people are still too few. We have the ability and the money to do as we like, but we do not have the freedom to pursue our own interests. The main source of today's frustration is in fact the lack of freedom.

Second, we must help people to develop the necessary skills and talents to meet the changing labor standards of the next century, when labor productivity will be paramount. As high productivity becomes increasingly valuable, Japanese men and women will be eager and able to have long working lives. We will need to make the best of their abilities. The emphasis will not be on people working themselves to the bone, reducing themselves body and soul to labor, but rather on investing their energies in their own health and development. People will therefore need the time and scope to pursue self-development.

Third, reduction of working hours is part of a broader-based international effort to coordinate work practices. Japan's working habits must meet international standards, particularly those of other advanced industrial nations. We must, therefore, reduce working hours to common-sense levels.

Let me qualify this by saying that I do not personally think that the Japanese work too hard. Europeans and Americans work with a high degree of concentration during working hours. They then leave when working hours are over and spend their free time with their families or pursuing their own interests. In Japan, though, work during working hours is often of a very low intensity (with the exception of assembly-line work). People work overtime instead. One might even say with some hyperbole that though the total amount of work accomplished is roughly the same, in one work culture, people finish the job within working hours, while in the other, they work long hours of overtime.

Sharing international standards of work styles is not simply a matter of reducing hours. It entails changing the way we work: we need greater intensity and concentration during working hours. The movement to shorten working days must embrace this broader change in work culture.

Naturally, income should not be reduced along with hours. As work will be done more efficiently, we have to change our notion of how income is calculated. Moreover, if we cut income and residence taxes in half, people should have plenty of money to live comfortable lives even without working overtime.

By calling for reduced working hours I by no means intend to send the message that Japanese should not work. Japan cannot possibly support itself without the continued will of the people to work, since we cannot rely on natural resources for our sustenance. The purpose of shortening working hours is to enable people to work intensively and eagerly during work hours and to spend their free time as they please.

The impact of reduced work hours will be enormous. First, the relationship between companies and labor will change fundamentally. Today, workers often feel that they live under a huge company umbrella. With the various benefits it provides, the company has seemed to many to be all there was in life. If we succeed in reducing working hours, people will be able to achieve some distance from the company, to find some space that will permit them to plan their own lives, select their own work, and develop their own abilities. The reduction of working hours has to be the first step in achieving "freedom from companies."

People will use their free time in countless ways. Some may want to take a holiday and rest from the fatigue of the working year. Other would undoubtedly spend the time to study and develop new skills. We complain that our children "study too hard," but it is the adults who really need to study. If people can take the time to upgrade their own abilities and broaden their understanding of the world around them rather than give themselves entirely to their companies, they will not "lack things to do" after retirement.

People in Europe and America often take vacations up to four weeks long. Many use this time to rest with their families in the countryside while also devoting some hours each day to language or other specialized study. Even in their regular working lives, many people pursue M.B.A.s and other degrees at night school. Unfortunately, Japanese today do not have that flexibility. Some may have the opportunity for such education as part of their company training programs. What is important is that people have the freedom to pursue the education they themselves feel they need.

Reduction of working hours will permit individuals to develop skills that will be valuable in their careers as well. During the catch-up years, when we knew with certainty what we needed to make and how to make it, people acquired the necessary techniques and knowledge from their predecessors on the shop floor. The longer they stayed in the company, the more skilled they became. But factory-based knowledge is no longer adequate for today's high-technology market needs. The decisive factors in success hereafter will be a keen sense for consumption trends, the theoretical grounding to analyze product ideas, and the creativity to design new products and markets.

Our best workers, then, will make time outside of work to educate themselves. People will have to study from the earliest stages of their careers if they wish to enjoy long working lives.

The increased free hours can also be used for activities that contribute to society. It is often said that international and social service activities are not highly developed in Japan. The reason for this is not that Japanese are less inclined than others to such activities, but that we simply do not have room in our lives for anything outside the company. A one- or two-year leave from the company to work in economic aid activities abroad, for example, would be invaluable for everyone concerned. Such overseas experiences enrich not only the lives of those who actually go abroad, but their companies and all of society as well.

Weekend service activities are also important. If people had the time and means, they could volunteer for environmental activities or for community and social service. These services cannot be sustained solely on the efforts of government; when welfare activities are reduced simply to collecting taxes and building old age homes or welfare facilities, they have no soul. Similarly, money alone is never enough. The growing demands on the system would simply increase the tax burden on everyone.

A dynamic welfare state requires the participation of the people. We cannot build a high-quality welfare society without contact and exchange among our citizens. Those who participate actively in social service efforts are especially aware of the enrichment that comes with these activities.

An 1800-Hour Work Year

My basic aims fall roughly into four categories: full use of paid vacations, time-and-a-half pay for overtime work, two-day weekends, and forty-hour workweeks. I call these goals "basic" for two reasons. First, these four conditions have already been met by advanced nations such as America and Britain, which have work years of roughly 1900 hours even though they have been relatively slow to accept shorter work hours. If Japan could reduce its work year to 1800 hours, we will have reached and even surpassed the standard they have set. Thus, the four aims I cited are minimum and basic.

The second reason is that these will be considered the basic conditions for future market competition. At some point, we will not be allowed to compete with other nations by foregoing two-day weekends and paid vacations. Rules are already being drawn up that will prohibit nations from competing on the basis of labor conditions that do not meet the standards shared by advanced nations.

The proportion of Japanese workers taking paid vacations finally exceeded 50 percent in the 1980s, but we still have a long way to go. The average vacation time even for those who do take it is usually a maximum of eight days, an especially low number next to America's twenty days and Germany's thirty days. Opinion polls show that the two main reasons why people do not take their paid vacations are 1) they fear "causing trouble for our colleagues if we take the day off," and 2) they want to "save up days in case we get sick."

Planned vacations, company rules for organizing them, and temporary labor services can go a long way toward eliminating the first concern. And it is truly unfortunate if people need to "save vacation days for sickness. " Most advanced countries have sick-leave systems in place. Japan, too, should make such provisions so that people do not have to use their holidays other than for the pleasure for which they were intended.

One effective way of encouraging people to take their holidays is to increase the number of national holidays. We might stretch the New Year's holiday to the seventh of January; designate all of the annual spring "Golden Week" a national holiday, including May 1; and declare another "Golden Week" in the fall. Every season could thus have an extended vacation period. This effectively means that the national government would be forcing holidays on the people by a kind of decree, but it may be the most promising approach in a nation where people are reluctant to plan their own holidays. To alleviate the traffic problems that arise when the entire nation takes its holiday on the same day, each prefecture or city could freely select its own public holidays.

However, it is the companies themselves that should take the initiative and increase the number of holidays they offer; they should also take steps to ensure that workers actually take these holidays, and preferably leave it up to workers to decide when they will take their time off. Government policy, meanwhile, should focus on spreading such efforts throughout society. We can arrange to publicize which companies give the most holidays, or reward companies that actively arrange days off for their workers.

Overtime pay will also prove extremely important for maintaining competitiveness. Labor hours should be adjusted to the strengths of the economy at any given time. Some industries may require longer hours, and some shorter. Working hours, in other words, should be set not uniformly but by the particular needs of each industry and each company. The best way to encourage companies to shorten working hours is to make overtime labor more costly. The government should not seek to interfere with the competitive advantages of individual companies; companies that want their workers to work long hours and are willing to pay time-and-a-half wages may do so.

In the coming labor shortage, small and medium-sized firms that cannot afford two-day weekends or shorter working hours will find it increasingly difficult to hire people. If forty-hour workweeks and two-day weekends are required by law, however, then all firms will have to adhere to the rules. All companies, large and small, will compete under the same conditions. This can only be to the benefit of small firms.

CHAPTER FIVE

Freedom from Ageism and Sexism

The Contributions of Senior Citizens

Japanese society is now aging at a pace unprecedented anywhere in the world.

The first concerns that come to mind when we think of senior citizens have to do with medical, pension, and social welfare facilities. These are extremely important, but I would like to consider the issue of the aging society in a different light.

The most crucial need of senior citizens is not the small pension they receive, but the zest for life that comes with contributing—as they have throughout their lives—to self, to family, and to society. In other words, it is most important to senior citizens that they not lose their freedom on account of their age; they, like everyone, need to continue to live a social existence. People need the freedom to work and the freedom to participate in society. Unfortunately, Japan's senior citizens today do not enjoy either of these.

No one escapes aging. Very soon, Japanese society will have the largest proportion of senior citizens in the world. We have no time to lose in putting our minds to the issues raised by an aging society. "Senior citizen" is a catch-all term that includes a vast range of people. Many senior citizens are ailing and do require social protection, but the majority are relatively healthy people with plenty of energy. As we live longer, the number of healthy senior citizens will grow. Our first priority must be the creation of an environment in which these senior citizens can actively participate in society.

If we are serious about eliminating the "three excesses" (children's excess study, excess work of adults, and excess free time for senior citizens), we must undertake a thoroughgoing social reform to rebuild our company-centered society, beginning with a reduction of working hours. We don't need to wait for a social revolution before we expand the opportunities for senior citizens to participate in society. There are plenty of policies available right now. The lifetime of experience that senior citizens have accumulated can be put to social use in many ways, and can thereby contribute to their own lives. For most people, active participation in society would mean being able to work in their own specialized areas. This is an important problem that I will address again later, so I will here discuss other areas in which senior citizens might be active.

• *Education.* Currently, only professional teachers are permitted to teach at the elementary, junior-high, and high-school levels. Their task is to impress upon the children whatever knowledge is called for in the Ministry of Education's "Outline of Educational Guidelines." However, in the effort to expand the choices available to adults, we must begin by diversifying the content of childhood education. Senior citizen participation in classrooms is one of the unique learning experiences we will have to offer children. The knowledge and experience senior citizens have to impart are undeniably a valuable part of education.

• *Technical training; aid programs.* Personnel contributions will only become more important in the international contributions Japan will make in the future. Since working people can only rarely take one-year leaves from their jobs to work on outside projects, the government should actively support the use of what is an excellent resource for international contributions—the abilities and experience of our senior citizens. Even now, many senior citizens offer technical and other assistance to communities overseas.

Recently, for example, retired specialists from a synthetic textiles factory in Hokuriku traveled to several Asian countries to offer technical instruction. If there were more opportunities to offer help on a paid basis as part of government programs, there is no question that many more people would offer their services.

• *Welfare.* As I mentioned above, most senior citizens in their sixties and seventies are very healthy. They are uneasy about their future health and understand better than anyone the importance of social services for senior citizens; they give serious consideration to the problems senior citizens face. It would be useful to arrange for "young" senior citizens to participate actively in welfare efforts. They might do so on a volunteer basis, but as long as they are offering their time, they should be able to earn some money. The government should give strong support to their work.

These three activities are just a few of the areas in which senior citizens can make valuable contributions. But such activities will have a hard time taking hold without policies to direct them. This is where the government comes in. It is far preferable to spend money on developing such programs and thereby to enable senior citizens to contribute to society and enjoy greater quality of life, than simply to pour money exclusively into welfare systems. Even more important, our senior citizens will discover renewed pride and meaning in their lives.

Senior Citizens in the Workplace

Japan's young labor force will begin to contract in 1995. By the year 2000, the overall work force will begin to shrink. It is becoming increasingly urgent that we begin preparing for the employment of senior citizens.

Japan's labor market has hitherto been molded by an employment system premised on permanent employment and seniority wage structures. This system, as I stressed earlier, lent tremendous power to Japan's rapid economic growth. Senior citizens, however, were left standing on the sidelines in this labor market.

The permanent employment system is already collapsing. Its collapse will not only expand the range of choices available to senior citizens but will be of great significance for Japanese industry itself as it develops employment opportunities for senior citizens. We are already beginning to see signs of such transformations of the permanent employment system, as more and more people change jobs and careers. Employment opportunities for senior citizens are increasing little by little, but the pace of change is very slow. If we leave things to work themselves out naturally, nothing will change fast enough to accommodate the pace of the aging of society or the coming labor shortage. A major responsibility for government, then, is to remove the obstacles senior citizens face in the workplace and actively promote their employment.

From the point of view of the senior citizen, the obstacles to work are low wages and poor working conditions. From the company's view, it is hard to use senior citizens effectively. Hiring and working methods lack flexibility on both sides of the labor-management relationship.

We must begin by promoting the practice of paying people according to their abilities and contributions. Senior citizens and young people with the same abilities should be paid the same hourly wage. Small businesses and craftsmen already give the same compensation for the same skills. Age is not a factor. Such a practice could act as an incentive to white-collar workers as well and offer them life-giving energy in their older years.

Skills present a different problem. Salaried workers today are usually shifted to managerial jobs as they grow older and are gradually removed from day-to-day operations. The skills they develop are personal, such as the ability to move the organization in the desired direction. Accordingly, when they transfer to other companies, or even to non-managerial jobs in the same firm, these skills are not transferable. Specialized skills offer the most promise of transferability. Workers must therefore maintain and upgrade these skills from the early stages of their careers.

However, to retrain older workers, we need policies with more immediate effect. Today's senior citizens worked very hard in their youth; there is no question that, with some additional skills, they can contribute significantly to day-to-day business operations. Companies hire so many young people that they have not had to learn how to use the considerable skills of their older workers; they let training and education for older workers fall behind.

A policy proposal that may apply here and be very effective would be to give substantial public assistance to companies that seek to educate, train, and employ senior workers. The policy could also apply to individuals who try to pursue their own training outside the company framework. The government can help by reducing the costs of such training through tax deductions and subsidies. We might also establish public education and training programs.

We must also make employment practices more flexible. As people age, it is natural that they should be reluctant to work long hours. Part- or half-time workers often suffer inferior working conditions, while companies find it hard to use their skills effectively. Many senior citizens would like very much to work if they could do so on a part-time or consulting basis where their skills are needed and put to good use. Special skills offered on a consultancy or part-time basis will become increasingly important to companies that need access to a wide range of professional expertise. It is rational for companies to rely on outside people for high-level skills that they only need from time to time.

Our biggest obstacle is our way of thinking. We will have to acknowledge that the distinctions we draw between part-time and full-time workers or between salaried workers and outside consultants are unrelated to quality issues. We should legislate a nondiscrimination principle to eliminate the discriminatory distinctions between part-time and full-time employees. I have in mind here the Part-time Law proposed by four of the opposition parties.* However, to establish part-timers as skilled and valuable employees, they must be made eligible for the same social insurance benefits and be subject to the same income taxes as full-time workers. This law will also be crucial for promoting the participation of women in the workplace, as I will discuss below.

If the conditions described above are met, senior citizens will be able to participate actively in society. It will, inevitably, take time to achieve these fundamental changes. Companies today assume they need not hire senior citizens. They neglect their training and rarely consider more flexible hiring practices. Under such circumstances, the hiring of senior citizens is not likely to make serious progress. Nor will governmental measures to ensure their employment make much headway.

We need to break this cycle. For the foreseeable future, we must require companies to retain people up to the age of sixty-five. This is essential in part because we will eventually have to raise the age at which people will begin receiving their pensions to sixty-five. People should not be required to work full-time beyond age sixty, however; contracts may be written for part-time or consultancy work in which workers maintain their hourly wages. Again, those who retire early or whose skills simply are not applicable to company needs should receive company pensions equivalent to part-time wages.

National and prefectural governments and public organizations should of course take the lead in implementing such plans in public workplaces, and do so as quickly as possible. Bureaucrats must lay the groundwork to ensure that the abilities of senior citizens are not wasted.

Increasing Choices for Women

Many of the employment problems of senior citizens apply equally to women. In a labor market premised on permanent employment, women, like senior citizens, are automatically relegated to the sidelines. This requires immediate attention, not only because of the economic challenge posed by the coming labor shortage, but also because we must offer greater scope and more diverse choices for women to fashion their own lives.

Childbearing and child-rearing have heretofore constituted major obstacles to women's participation in the workplace. It is impossible to exaggerate the importance of the work women have done in the home, but it is women who should choose whether they wish to be confined to the home. A wider range of roles and opportunities must be offered to women. At the same time, men, senior citizens, and children will have to help out more with the household work.

Japan's labor market is still shaped by the uniform assumption that men go outside to work while women maintain the home. The permanent employment system hinders women, as it hinders senior citizens, from entering the work force. As with senior citizens, conditions are changing bit by bit, but the pace is much too slow. Without reforms imposed from the outside—through government policy—we will not see significant changes anytime soon.

There are a number of concrete policy options available to us. Let me touch on the major points that need to be addressed. We must first build the social support systems that will permit women to pursue both careers and homemaking. Policies should stress the strengthening of company maternity-leave plans. We must also expand systems to allow for childcare and assistance in homemaking. The costs need not all be borne publicly, but we must, at a minimum, establish effective and reliable institutions to perform these functions. This does not mean, of course, that we should attach less value to the burden of homemaking and child-rearing. The work done in the home, including child-rearing first and foremost, will only become more important in the future. The responsibility should therefore not be placed entirely on women: men, too, should have support structures that will enable them to play active roles in the domestic arena.

Second, as our society ages, the care of elderly people will also become an increasingly serious problem. Like child-rearing, this has become almost exclusively the responsibility of women. Women in their forties and fifties who have worked hard to develop and sustain long-term careers frequently find themselves resigning from their jobs to care for elderly parents, either their own or their husband's.

Leaving work in mid-career does even more damage to women's careers than taking time for child-rearing at a younger age. Women who take some years early in adult life to raise children can eventually reenter the workplace. As the children grow, women gain some free time, often enough to enable them to return to work. Ultimately, of course, childcare ends altogether. In contrast, the burden of caring for the elderly only becomes heavier with time. It is impossible to know if or when a woman will be free to do other work. It is a serious loss from both an economic and a social point of view to have experienced and responsible career women in their peak working years be forced to leave their jobs.

The government must therefore give public assistance for the care of the elderly and for the care of children. Caregivers could assist the elderly in their homes rather than consign them to hospitals. The national government could hire home caregivers and assist elderly people in bearing the costs of the special facilities they will need in their homes. The education and development of manpower to handle home care is itself becoming an urgent policy issue. We must build a society in which women can both fulfill their filial obligations and work outside the home in satisfying positions if they so desire.

Providing Pensions to Housewives

Women who leave their companies to raise families fall behind their male colleagues in skill and experience. This is true even where companies invest in women's education and training. Lacking the background for higher-level work, they are given only simple tasks to do when they come back to the workplace after several years. The problem may best be addressed first by requiring companies to give men and women the same education and training, and second by easing the cost burden on companies through tax and other incentives. The maintenance and upgrading of women's skills are essential for the participation of women in the workplace.

Just as with senior citizens, it is vital that Japan adopt more diverse work and hiring styles if women are going to be able to enter the workplace. We need not insist that husbands work full-time while wives work part-time and do the housework. We need an environment where husbands can perform high-level work on a part-time basis and also work at home if we want to enable women to work outside the home more readily. We need policies, in other words, that will expand the choices available in work and hiring practices.

Reform of the permanent employment system is another policy area that is crucial for women's participation in society. Most public workplaces like teacher organizations, city offices, insurance offices, and hospitals guarantee permanent employment as a matter of principle. This means that it is, in principle, impossible to become an elementary school teacher in mid-career. It is obviously important that teachers have experience, but there is no reason that every teacher must have acquired that experience in his or her twenties. There is no reason why well-educated women cannot begin teaching in schools in their forties, after they have raised their own families. Fresh blood of this kind could improve the level of education, not undermine it.

Permanent employment has become a meaningless principle in many cases of public hiring. It is discriminatory to hire only young people. I believe we can induce momentous changes throughout Japan's labor market by implementing our reforms in public offices, hospitals, and insurance offices.

The difficulties faced by women resemble those of senior citizens in other ways. Because companies have not hired women as regular workers, none of the groundwork has been laid for doing so. Again, we probably need temporary measures requiring that women be hired.

We must begin by implementing these measures in all public-sector jobs. The civil service—originally intended to reflect the composition of the citizenry—is composed overwhelmingly of males. Neither the bureaucracy nor the Diet reflect the population they serve. A certain proportion of women in the public workplace should be required by law. This is not an ideal solution, but it may be a useful provisional measure until the hiring of women becomes established practice.

I want to emphasize here that the work women do in the household is extremely important. The unfortunate truth of the Japanese system is that we maintain obstacles against women who want to work outside the home, and at the same time deprecate the work women do at home. It is surely as important to bear and raise the next generation of Japanese, to do the housework, and sustain family life, as it is to work outside the house for wages.

Widows' pensions reflect this contradiction. Women who have worked outside the home receive their own full pensions even when their husbands die. This is as it should be, but widowed housewives receive only half the pension. The difference is unwarranted. Under our current pension system, the pensions that senior citizens receive do not come out of monies they have paid in over the years, but out of taxes paid by today's young working people. Yet the housewives who raised these young people receive only half the pension of working women, who may or may not have raised children. This contradicts the basic principle governing our pension system. Housewives and their husbands clearly constitute a single unit. The housewife bearing the responsibility for housework and child-rearing is contributing to society, just as her working husband is. When her husband dies, the wife should naturally have full rights to his pension.

* "Opposition parties" refers to those under the LDP government.

Freedom from Regulations

Anachronistic Regulations

I recently had occasion to hear a discussion of land prices in a certain regional city. The city has an urban district at its center, a "controlled urbanization district" outside of that, and an "agriculture promotion district" on the periphery. Land in the residential areas most recently developed in the urban district costs roughly ¥600,000 per *tsubo* (36 sq. feet), while land in the "controlled" district costs about ¥200,000 per *tsubo*. The "agriculture promotion" land at the very outskirts, which might be expected to be least expensive of all, runs at roughly ¥400,000 per *tsubo*.

Why do such peculiarities arise? The controlled urbanization district neighboring the city center became the object of strict regulations because it was feared that it would face intense development pressures. The regulations sought to protect farmlands in the controlled area by restricting almost all development except that by younger sons of farmers. Meanwhile, the agriculture promotion district that was also intended to protect farmland is subject to almost no regulation, because no one expected residential development to press that far into the hinterland. But residential development has leapfrogged the controlled district into the agriculture promotion districts, with the result that prices climbed to the ¥400,000 level.

Ironically, the agricultural district that was supposed to preserve

197

the best land for farming is the one being developed most intensively; land prices there have risen steadily despite its location. The
farmland in the controlled district is meanwhile the area's most
protected land. Clearly, urban planning of this kind is badly
managed. It has not even succeeded in preserving the best farmland.

No one—urban planners or anyone else—foresaw the spread of
automobiles. No one imagined that people would be able to drive
from the country into the city within thirty minutes. Urban planning chugged along without recognizing that motorization was the
definitive development of our times.

If policy making cannot predict these kinds of changes, it must
at least be able to make rapid shifts in policy so as to assure, in this
case, for example, both urban development and protection of good
farmland. This is only possible if regulations undergo periodic
review. But the unfortunate regulations in this regional city simply
stayed on the books, and planning went nowhere. Aggressive
efforts should be made to change regulations as times change. This
cannot be done in Japan today.

I am not saying that regulations are altogether superfluous.
Currently, however, new regulations are simply tacked onto out-
dated regulations that are preserved in their original form until
every aspect of citizens' lives is bound by regulations. A liberal
society should be founded on laissez-faire principles. Only the
minimum necessary regulations should be maintained.

The excessive number of anachronistic regulations constrains
the lives of people on every front. Urban planning and other problems are not unique to the area I described; they are ubiquitous.
Meaningless regulations tie up our lives in issues related to transport, finance, distribution, and land use. They distort our lives. To
build a truly liberal society, and to make our lives more pleasant,
we must immediately commence deregulation.

Toward a Rule-Based Administration

Problems like those faced in urban planning can be found in
many areas. Public works, for example, are allocated according to

detailed standards determined by the central government and carried out uniformly nationwide. The result is that the entire country has the same community centers and public halls, but it is doubtful whether any given region actually receives the specific kind of public investment it needs.

Again, central planning for the encouragement of industry is channeled through prefectural governments and carried out in tandem as directed. Kasumigaseki stands at the center of industrial policy making, while the *raison d'être* of the prefectures is to loyally carry out its directives. Industry, however, differs from place to place; industrial policy should be specific to the region in question.

A factory analogy would place the role of Kasumigaseki in postwar Japan to that of foreman. MITI (Ministry of International Trade and Industry), the Ministry of Finance, and other agencies decided how to allocate industrial capital and circulated funds to the areas they chose. The bureaucracy responsible for transportation similarly determined how much should be allocated to which district, and set prices. It managed everything from the assignment of taxi districts to the allocation of airline flight routes to the certification of truck transport businesses. Similarly, the Ministry of Education set educational guidelines (aimed especially at the elementary level) and decided where to establish district schools and how to divide the children and teachers among them. As foreman, Kasumigaseki managed the large factory called Japan.

I acknowledge that this factory-management approach was a crucial engine for rapid economic growth, and that it had obvious value as such. There is no question that the concentrated—if too uniform—power of the administrative system was able to absorb foreign technology in a short span of time and thereby succeeded in raising the Japanese economy to world-leading levels. But management of this kind became untenable as the "factory" that is the Japanese economy grew too big. The actual economy is a fluid entity and not something that can be managed by a handful of administrative organizations. People's needs change radically, as does technology. Most importantly, if the life of the citizenry is to be subjugated to a single image of the ideal society, what becomes of freedom?

The failings of management-style administration are clearly revealed in the travails of our financial administration, which recently attracted attention with the collapse of the bubble economy. Every aspect of the finance industry, from the building of new bank branches to the establishment of deposit interest rates, was carried out under the strict regulation and supervision of the Ministry of Finance. For regulatory purposes, finance was not only divided by sector—into banks, securities, and insurance—but was subdivided further so that the banking sector alone included long- and short-term finance, the savings banks, and other narrow regulatory divisions. The ministry also gave detailed guidance in every action taken by individual financial organs. Again, we return to the image of the foreman managing his factory.

The consequences of this approach are becoming clear. The premise underlying close administration of this kind was that the money market would remain a manageable size and that there would be no great change in existing conditions. In reality, the capital market became increasingly global, complex, and diverse. The changes were significant and constant, and the ministry "overlords" simply could not manage the details across so wide a territory. The financial industry survived under MOF administrative protection, but since the "overlords" could not supervise everything under their jurisdiction, financial institutions and non-banks came to suffer extensive bad debts. Serious crimes took place in the banking industry.

The administration of the financial industry must be changed from the bottom up. It should not become an entirely unregulated industry. My argument is that we must replace management-through-regulation with rule-based policies. In other words, we should stop using regulations to check company activities before they take place, and instead have policies designed to contain any undesirable results of the action taken by companies.

Companies, Individuals, and Responsibility

We must manage company behavior through the power of the market, not the power of the bureaucrat. We can ensure greater opportunities for consumers if we insist on strict corporate disclosure.

We must determine, for example, precisely what rules the financial industry should follow and subject the industry to strict scrutiny. Rules might include maintaining a certain capital-to-assets ratio; limiting excessive real estate financing; or requiring healthy risk-management standards. We must make the industry as transparent as possible through public disclosure of conditions in financial organizations.

With conditions like these firmly in place, consumers will have to take responsibility for their own choices. People will be able to use their own judgment to strike a balance between risk and return, select the appropriate financial institutions or products, and take responsibility for whatever results ensue. In essence, this will mean that financial institutions are guided by the actions of their customers. Bureaucratic administration will naturally be responsible for determining whether or not financial institutions are strictly observing the rules, and violators should be subject to harsh penalties.

This shift from management-type regulation to rule-based policies should not be limited to the financial sector; it can be equally applied to the monopolistic practices of companies. Japan's Anti-Monopoly Law, for example, includes many exceptions to the rules, as America has recently charged. Between the legally recognized exceptions to this law and the cases that are considered not to be subject to the law, numerous sectors of our economy avoid application of the law.

Specific industries each come under the jurisdiction of a particular bureaucracy. This makes it difficult to broadly apply general rules like the Anti-Monopoly Law. Finance is administered by the Ministry of Finance, steel and autos by MITI, transportation by the

Transport Ministry, broadcasting by the Ministry of Posts and Telecommunications, and pharmaceuticals by the Health Ministry. Vertical administration of this kind is unavoidable to a degree, but it has become so restrictive that it obstructs free competition. Instead of directly controlling company activities, we should enforce rules like the Anti-Monopoly Law to restrain them.

We of course need rules governing product safety (especially in medicine), public ownership of broadcast or financial networks, and many other areas. We must ensure the transparency of such rules and keep management-type administration to a minimum.

Privatization must also continue if we are to utilize the knowledge and ideas of the private sector. Japan Railways (JR), Nippon Telephone and Telegraph (NTT), and Japan Tobacco (JT) privatization efforts still have some way to go, but they do constitute progress in the privatization of public corporations. By privatizing, we will upgrade the efficiency and quality of services and reduce the financial burden on national and local governments, and thus free public funding for projects that truly require it. The government must scrap and build just as private companies do. Areas that the government no longer needs to manage should be delegated to the private sector, and government activity should shift its focus to those areas where it is truly appropriate. A thorough study of sectors to be privatized should be carried out as quickly as possible.

CHAPTER SEVEN

Establishing Real Freedom

Democracy and Citizen Autonomy

I cannot help but feel that the biggest source of our lack of freedom lies with the people. In other nations, democracy began with the revolt of citizens who demanded rights from their king or overlord. Democracy is the self-rule of citizens and is premised on the idea that citizens can stand on their own feet and take responsibility for themselves. As long as citizens are unable or unwilling to take responsibility for themselves, we will have only a quasi-democracy, no matter how much politicians and bureaucrats strive to institute democratic practices.

Postwar Japan ostensibly adopted American-style democracy, but the people have been robbed of their freedom. This may be due in part to the survival of the prewar bureaucratic system, but more fundamentally it is because the conditions for democracy were not met by the citizens.

The prewar Imperial military forces were one of the best-trained, best-disciplined, and strongest in the world. However, although the soldiers were excellent as parts in a large organization, they were not autonomous individuals. They did not have their own values and could not act on their own judgment. Japan's defeat revealed this, but in historical terms, it was only a momentary event. It could not possibly bring fundamental changes to the Japanese character.

With the prerequisites for democracy missing, American-style "postwar democracy" could not take root. It has not taken root, even to this day. This is the fundamental reason why Japanese society lacks freedom today. Postwar education, which set out to lay the groundwork for democracy, in fact worked in diametric opposition to its supposed mission. Today, we see the signs of this failing in the spread of violence in the school and home, of drugs, AIDS, and the destructive behavior of our youth. No one can seriously argue that education is not implicated in these problems.

To see true liberty in Japanese society, we must embark upon bold education reforms. There are many weaknesses in education, but we must first confront the problems at the elementary and secondary levels. Japanese education at this level is given high marks abroad, and indeed, according to the International Association for the Evaluation of Educational Achievement (IEA), Japanese students rank in the highest levels. America, conversely, ranks close to the bottom. The contrast between the two is a constant subject of discussion. This does not mean, however, that our elementary and secondary education cannot be improved.

In fact, the seeds of autonomy and subjectivity in Japanese children are discouraged from developing under the current education system. An American cultural anthropologist who once surveyed Japanese high school students described them as follows. The students, as he saw them, have their feet bound by the examination system. The path before them lies straight and very narrow. They are completely restricted by their families and schools. Those who do not follow this path are penalized.

He found that they are encouraged not to attempt new things but to adapt themselves to the reality around them. They are taught to favor external appearance over their internal selves. They believe that they must deny their own selves and adhere strictly to the surface order of things. They do not learn to express their thoughts. They are not encouraged to talk or to write. They are not trained to think or to debate. They do not even learn that there is more than one way to interpret a single issue. Memorization takes priority over analysis, and the official curriculum places little or no emphasis on the students' artistic natures, their personalities, or their humanity.

I agree with the anthropologist's conclusions. Today's high school students are urged only to cram themselves with information. The same is true of elementary and junior high school education. I understand that teachers in America and Britain begin discussion by agreeing with children's statements, then probe their reasoning and assumptions and begin to argue other points of view. Teachers encourage them, and at the same time foster the children's ability to think for themselves. By contrast, teachers in Japanese classrooms always have the right answers, which are duly absorbed by the children. The teacher calls on one child after another until he hears the right answer to his question, at which point he moves on to the next question. The class is taught as if by computers, though conducted by flesh-and-blood teachers.

From elementary school to high school, children busily cram themselves with the correct answers. They go all the way to college without polishing their skills or developing the habit of thinking for themselves. This cannot possibly produce autonomous citizens. Clearly, our educational practices are not entirely mistaken, nor are those of America or Europe necessarily correct. However, the question we are addressing is why democracy has not taken root in Japan. Surely the differences between Japanese and Western education account for part of the answer.

Education that Encourages Independent Thinking

We must begin tackling elementary and junior high school education by reforming the standardized guidance of education from the center. We should replace our uniform national education curriculum with one divided between basic academic skills and applied studies. The former should be directed by the central government; the latter should come under the jurisdiction of education committees established by local governments.

Basic academic skills here refer to the 3R's. The central government must establish standards for the basic skills that students must acquire by certain ages. It is responsible for assuring that the entire population meets those standards. However, it should delegate to regional governments responsibility for the precise curricula by which such standards are to be met, as well as the content of social studies and science curricula. This would enable each area to root its education in its own culture; it would help develop a diverse population. If the various districts are allowed some autonomy in education, Japan's teachers will no longer be forced to teach only one way of understanding things.

Such a modification would render the system of standardized national examinations untenable. The nature of entrance exams will accordingly have to change, which will in turn help remove the emphasis on cramming in the junior high years.

I am not suggesting that any central government guidance of education is a mistake. It is clear from IEA test results that this form of education is efficient. It unquestionably served postwar Japan's rapid economic growth. But we also lost a great deal in the process.

Not only did democracy not take root, regional autonomy declined. The center maintained a monopoly on information. People became apathetic about the financing of education. Problems were left to fester because those in charge locally lacked the skills to address them. Parents, schools, and local school districts lost authority over education until finally they were no longer equipped to assume responsibility for it. If the schools themselves have no sense of themselves as the actors in education, they have no way of teaching students to perceive themselves that way.

We also need to consider the fact that children are maturing earlier than they used to. We will probably want to lower the age at which students enter school. The majority of students continue their education until high school; we might want to consider making attendance compulsory all the way to that level. If we integrate junior high and high schools, entrance exams prior to high school should not be necessary. Elimination of junior high exams would alleviate at least some of the exam competition.

Higher education, too, needs reform. Japanese university education is not highly regarded either at home or abroad. One of the biggest reasons for this is the lack of appetite for study among college students. Since exam competition ends with entrance into university, people regard admittance as an almost automatic passport into society.

Students also find the classes dull because the character of the university itself is ambiguous. Historically, Japan's national universities were divided between those that offered high-level academic educations, like the Imperial universities, and professional/vocational schools that trained people in specific occupations. Private universities provided liberal educations, primarily for future white-collar workers. With time, however, this division broke down. In the postwar period, Japan recklessly eliminated any distinctions and turned them all into the same kind of university. The purposes of university education have become too vague.

The universities must clarify their particular aims and characteristics, including general liberal education, professional education, and academic research. We need an education system that can better respond to the needs of the times.

On Teaching

Finally, I would like to touch on the question of teachers' status in society. Teachers are the most important influence, after parents, on the growth of children. Just as parents do not regard the education of their children as a nine-to-five job, neither should teachers. Education is qualitatively different from office work or the production of goods.

Teachers therefore should not have the right to strike or the right to union negotiations that belong to other laborers. Teachers do have unions in advanced democratic nations, but teacher unions in Britain, for example, aim toward the development of the professional abilities of teachers. The aim in Japan, by contrast, is simply to defend teachers' rights as laborers.

This "labor consciousness" of teachers needs to be erased so that teachers can more honestly undertake their jobs as educators of our children. The "three rights of labor" should not apply for teachers. Instead, teachers must be given the social status of "special civil servants."

Education cannot be considered in isolation from its relationship with society. Society gives rise to today's education, and vice-versa. Each is both the cause and effect of the other. It is therefore difficult to know where to begin to solve problems. We must start where we can, and a ripple effect will follow.

Our lives are changing dramatically in these last years of the twentieth century. Individual Japanese desire a more affluent life. Japan's political leadership thus bears a great responsibility. The very roots of Japan's structures and lifestyles—hitherto taken for granted—must now be reviewed and, where necessary, revised. This is true even where the difficulties of doing so are daunting.

The reform of Japan does not belong only to Japan. Japan will only be able to fulfill its responsibilities in international society when people overseas can look at us and say, "We do want to be like the Japanese."

We must reform not only those policies immediately at hand, but those at the very root of today's social constructs. All our citizens must seriously consider for themselves what road they think we must travel to become a truly affluent society.

Pain will naturally accompany these reforms; no change is possible without some distress. Yet people undergo surgery in the knowledge that some pain is worth the promise of a fuller, better life. We endure difficulties today because we wish to bequeath an affluent society to our children and grandchildren.